THE
ASPEN
DAYHIKER

Ruth and Peter Frey

Brush Creek Books

BRUSH CREEK BOOKS
1317 Livingston Street
Evanston, Illinois 60201

Cover and illustrations by Donna Currier
Book design by Rivera Design & Communications

ISBN# 0-9636187-0-9

Printed in the United States of America

Dedication

To our friends in the Aspen chapter of the Colorado Mountain Club whose enthusiasm and boundless good cheer have brightened our summers, and especially to Jack de Pagter for his selfless leadership and encouragement.

Contents

Preface

The summer visitor to Aspen often arrives with a surplus of energy and a yen for adventure. Before setting forth into the wilderness, however, the would-be mountaineer should be realistic about readiness. The Elk Mountains are a place of joy and magic for those who are properly prepared. But the high country can be unpleasant and dangerous for the ambitious newcomer armed only with enthusiasm. Take time to learn about your proposed journey.

THE ASPEN DAYHIKER is our attempt to help others travel the mountains in comfort and safety. This guide summarizes the knowledge we have gleaned from kindred spirits in the Colorado Mountain Club; from people who have written eloquently of the outdoors; from novice hikers whose troubles we have encountered on the trails; and from our own journeys through Aspen's alpine neighborhoods.

While many hiking guides are written with backpackers in mind, we emphasize a dayhiking approach because we believe there are significant advantages. Dayhikers are less likely than backpackers to leave a permanent imprint on the wilderness; they pass through briefly, erecting no tents, building no fires, and doing minimal damage to the fragile vegetation. Dayhikers need not acquire the expensive items needed for an outdoor overnight. Dayhikers, even when fully-equipped, do not resemble heavily-laden pack animals. And dayhikers, at the close of the day, return to steamy showers, hot tubs, fresh clothing, dining options, and comfortable beds.

This handbook provides comprehensive descriptions of some of our favorite dayhikes. Additionally, it relays information about what to wear, what to carry, what to eat and drink, and what to expect from the elevation and the weather. **Please read these sections before you embark on your first trail**. The latter portion of the book offers an introduction to the wildlife, wildflowers, and trees you are likely to see in the Aspen area.

The dayhikes we have chosen range from three miles to twenty-three miles round trip in length. All involve elevation gain, and all require proper foot gear and a supply of water. They are grouped by length and difficulty.

The half-day hikes are suitable for most active families. A steady but unhurried pace and energy snacks for children are recommended. The hikes taking three-quarters of a day are more demanding and require more preparation. Late sleepers should pass these up, and some are not for young children. The full-day hikes are right for small groups committed to a brisk pace and furnished with adequate supplies. People badly out of shape should not attempt such strenuous workouts.

Finally, we present several very long dayhikes, appropriate only for those few zealots not adverse to physical pain. Do not even think about these unless you are in excellent shape and are thoroughly acclimated to the high country. On these trips it is essential to carry foul weather gear and extra equipment should you be injured and unable to reach your destination before nightfall.

As you sample these wonderful trails, remember that you are both a visitor to the wilderness and a caretaker of this federal land. Bring enthusiasm tempered with sensitivity. Tred lightly as you go. Leave undisturbed the beauty that you discover. And carry nothing with you that you do not carry away. The custody of wilderness is a personal responsibility.

"We do not inherit the land from our parents — we borrow it from our children."

Ruth and Peter Frey
March 1993

Getting Started

"
...at daybreak I am the sole
owner of all the acres I can walk over. It is not only
the boundries that disappear, but also the thought
of being bounded."

—Aldo Leopold

Getting Started

YOU HAVE SURELY KNOWN THE URGE TO JUST DO IT—TO SUCCUMB TO impulse, to chuck all the rules, to charge off into the inviting unknown. But in the mountains, there is wisdom in tempering fervor and in planning for adventure. Planning does not eliminate unexpected thrills. There will be plenty of excitement for both the cautious and the bold.

Preparation for alpine hiking begins before you arrive in Aspen. Good physical condition cannot be purchased at the mountaineering store; you must bring it with you. A regular exercise routine and attention to diet allow you to be more than a tourist. Once here, increase physical activity gradually to allow your body to adapt to the low air pressure of high altitude. An unhappy bout of mountain sickness could be your punishment for too much too soon.

Your first days should also include an increase in consumption of liquids. Drink more and drink often to fend off dehydration and related mountain sickness. Go easy on caffeine, a drying agent. And do not drink alcohol as it retards adaptation to high altitude. Foods high in carbohydrates require less oxygen for digestion, thereby fostering acclimation. Eating such foods additionally fuels the body for the sustained exercise of a hike.

Aspen, Snowmass, and the Roaring Fork Valley are wealthy with diversions. Sample them while you adjust. Acclimation days can give you time to read the pages of nature guides, to collect any gear that you lack, and to study trail descriptions and maps. Learn as much as you can about your route and destination. Note elevation gain and mileage. Assess the abilities of members of your party. Then choose your first excursion with care to enhance your experience among these splendid valleys and peaks.

Once you feel ready and have selected a hike, a few additional preparations will increase your enjoyment. The evening before any wilderness excursion is the time for an energy-loaded dinner and for selection of trail chow for the next day. Pack gear and dry foods, and refrigerate your bottles of water, fruits, etc. Inform a non-participant of your intended route and approximate time of return. Arrange a departure hour and meeting place with your hiking companions.

Finally, set your alarm clock for early rising. This may contradict your notion of vacation recreation. But fickle afternoon weather can spoil a good time. And above the trees, lightning is frightening. Plan to reach your goal before thunderclouds assemble. Remember, too, that intense mountain sunshine can diminish stamina. It is helpful to climb in the cool, invigorating early day. There are other advantages as well: wildlife sightings are more likely and insects are less aggressive. An early start also leads to a timely return; late afternoon in town offers music concerts and other pleasant distractions. Aspen's marriage of nature and culture is its summertime charm.

Potential Hazards

"*Just as a universe is violently constructed with a subtle beauty of form, mountains born of fire and force portray a similar magnificence.*"

—Immanuel Kant

Potential Hazards

WHILE THE MOUNTAIN ENVIRONMENT HAS MANY PERILS, IT IS MERCIfully free of some familiar problems. Snakes and spiders inject no venom, and meadows and forests are without poison oak and poison ivy. Damp, woodsy places do harbor mosquitoes, and biting flies are an occasional annoyance. But many trails are without either pest.

Giardia

Beautiful mountain streams and lakes have been invaded by a debilitating parasite, **Giardia lamblia**. This nasty organism, spread by mammalian feces, causes extreme intestinal distress and can be difficult to conquer. Campers can kill Giardia by boiling water for a minimum of 15 minutes. Dayhikers would be wise to carry adequate liquid or to pack purifying pumps or chemicals, both available at outdoor sports equipment stores. **Never drink untreated water.** Its sparkling clarity is deceptive.

Thunderstorms

The Colorado mountains are infamous for their summer storms. Often the day dawns with blue skies and a few innocuous, white cloud puffs. By late morning the clouds increase in size and number. By early afternoon the clouds thicken, turn gray, and dominate the sky. Suddenly the wind rises, the sky darkens, the temperature plummets 20 or 30 degrees, and rain, hail, and lightning descend. The hail can be large and dangerous. If you are on an open ridge or exposed in an alpine meadow above treeline, lightning can be lethal. If you do not have rain gear, the combination of wet clothes, strong wind, and cold temperatures can produce hypothermia, itself an insidious killer.

When planning an excursion above treeline, experienced dayhikers routinely arrive at the trailhead shortly after sunrise. An early start allows them to reach the high point of their journey by noon. If the sky is blue, they can linger on a mountain peak or in a high flowery meadow. If clouds build and the sky darkens, they have time to descend into the trees before the afternoon storm arrives.

Sometimes bad weather can arrive stealthily, emerging from behind a nearby peak. If you are caught above treeline in an electrical storm, crouch in a dry spot beside something higher than yourself. Do not touch rocks and avoid damp gullies as they both conduct electrical currents. Summer storms are often brief and, with luck, the danger will quickly pass. Rather than depend upon luck, however, you should keep a watchful eye on the sky. When the blue patches disappear, it is time to leave the high country.

Mountain Sickness

At eight thousand feet air pressure is 25 percent lower than at sea level. This decrease means that less oxygen is pushed into your lungs, and less oxygen reaches the cells that require it. Your body's natural reaction is to compensate for the lean air by increasing heart rate and respiration. After a few days your body begins to make physiological changes for more efficient absorption of available oxygen, but in the interim the struggle to adapt may produce symptoms of mild mountain sickness.

This malady takes 16 to 24 hours to develop and its symptoms vary in intensity by individual, by exertion level, by rate of ascent, and by altitude attained. Visitors who drive rather than fly to Aspen begin to adjust on the trip. Though mountain sickness has been reported at 6,500 feet of elevation, it is more likely at 8,000 feet and common at 10,000 feet. Sufferers notice a mild headache, nasal congestion, insomnia, loss of appetite, or breathlessness when climbing stairs or exercising. For most visitors such reactions signal only the need for time to acclimate. For a few the symptoms progress to serious illnesses that require emergency medical treatment.

While headache, the most frequent complaint, can be treated with aspirin or acetaminophen, strategies exist to avert or to minimize mountain sickness. The most uniformly recommended strategy is to eat lightly and to increase fluid consumption. Dehydration is a problem for everyone in a dry, high environment, and newcomers are especially vulnerable as their bodies excrete more urine in adjusting to altitude.

Other coping behaviors include moderate exercise and deep breathing to increase the body's uptake of oxygen. A diet emphasizing carbohydrates is helpful since carbohydrate foods require less oxygen for digestion and are easier on an unsettled stomach. Avoidance of alcohol and caffeine, both diuretics, is an excellent strategy for the first 48 to 72 hours. Alcohol, additionally, can slow acclimation by contributing to oxygen debt. Excessive alcohol may also contribute to high-altitude cerebral edema and high-altitude pulmonary edema, both life-threatening results of severe mountain sickness.

Individuals little troubled by altitude when in town may find that on the trail the combination of higher elevation, greater exertion, and dehydration conspire to stress the body. Mild symptoms, over the course of a challenging climb, can evolve into serious mountain sickness. This stage incorporates several of the following miseries: severe headache, nausea, vomiting, lassitude, dizziness, breathlessness at rest, loss of coordination and judgment, reduced urine output, swelling of face or extremities, and uncontrollable euphoria.

This is the time to listen to your body. Do not ignore your discomforts as they can develop into grave illnesses. **Descend**; it is the one certain cure. Drink liberal quantities of fluid. Hold mouth and nose tightly closed while pushing to drive air from lungs; this "pressure breath" forces more oxygen into the blood.

Physical conditioning, while ultimately important to the enjoyment of alpine hiking, seems to have no influence on an individual's susceptibility to mountain sickness. Response to altitude is very personal. Men and women are equally affected while younger people appear more at risk than their older companions. Individuals with a history of heart, circulatory, or lung disease should check with their physicians before visiting the high country.

Peripheral edema, a painless swelling of the face or hands, and more rarely
of the ankles or feet, is caused by fluid retention and/or abnormal fluid
distribution. Facial swelling is a sign of high altitude sickness. Edema of the
hands, the most common form, is not a reliable indicator. Hand swelling
is usually caused by the dangling, swinging motion of the arms, by
compression from backpack straps, or by cold or heat. If hands swell,
remove rings to prevent loss of the blood supply to fingers. Hands will
return to normal within a few hours after descending.

Hypothermia

When you venture far from the trailhead, there is always the possibility
that a sudden storm or a fall into a stream or lake can leave you wet and
cold. This is a dangerous situation. The threat is hypothermia, a decrease
in the temperature of the body's vital inner core. The combination of
wetness and wind can be lethal, especially in the coolness of the higher
elevations.

Hypothermia's warning signs are more easily detected by companions
than by the victim. Violent shivering, stumbling, slurred speech, and fuzzy
thinking progress to muscular rigidity, jerky motions, amnesia, hallucina-
tions, and lack of comprehension. If no corrective action is taken, the
victim becomes irrational, drifts into a stupor, loses consciousness, and as
the core temperature falls below 78 degrees, suffers failure of all vital
functions. Death can occur within a few hours of initial exposure to cold,
wetness, and wind.

As soon as you are aware of the potential danger, move quickly to conserve
the victim's body heat. Replace any wet clothing with dry garments. Find
a location that is sheltered from the wind. Cover the head, neck, and
hands. Restrict heavy exertion because body heat is lost from rapid
breathing and from perspiration. Contact with rocks, ice, or snow also
steals body heat. If possible, start a fire in a protected spot. Insulate the
victim from the ground, offer sweet foods and warm liquids if available,
and huddle other hikers around for heat transfer. If a sleeping bag is at
hand, place the hypothermia victim inside with another hiker.

The best prevention is careful preparation. Always bring extra clothing on
long trips, eat well before you set out, snack regularly to deliver heat and

energy, and carry a cigarette lighter or waterproof matches should you need to start a fire. Do not overestimate your capabilities or those of a companion. If you do not have the proper clothing to deal with wetness or cold, be willing to turn back.

Other Concerns

In June and early July picturesque **creeks and snow** can be deep and deceptive. Mountain snowmelt creates swift, icy torrents plunging toward valleys. Slippery rocks on stream bottoms complicate crossings. Some fords are difficult in mid-summer and impossible earlier. Wait a few weeks. Waterflow will diminish, and then you have a chance of staying dry and unhurt. Snow can festoon high passes into July. Drifts may disguise depressions and ledges, and large snowfields may hide tunnels of rushing snowmelt. Circumvent the deep stuff, or wait for it to vanish.

Ticks carrying Colorado tick fever are usually active from April until June and dwell among tall grasses and low shrubs. The virus they transmit produces severe flu-like symptoms of fever, fatigue, muscle pains, and headaches. Bedrest and analgesics are prescribed. Reasonable defenses are long sleeves, pants tucked into socks, a hat, regular tick inspections, and insect repellent. If these fail, pull embedded ticks slowly from the skin using tweezers, a handkerchief, or a tissue.

Though some lovely wildflowers are poisonous, few hikers are likely to eat them. But bare-legged trekkers can suffer brief, acute irritations from contact with **stinging nettles** (*Urtica gracilis*). Growing near creeks and irrigation ditches, these green spindly plants have sharply serrate opposite leaves and brittle stinging hairs that break when touched. The irritant substance includes acetylcholine and histamine.

Sustenance

"I live not in myself, but I become part of that around me: and to me high mountains are a feeling, but the hum of human cities torture."

—Lord Byron

Sustenance

Fluids

I F YOU HAVE BEEN EXCESSIVELY THIRSTY SINCE ARRIVING IN THE MOUNTAINS, you are experiencing **dehydration**, common in dry air anywhere and a special problem at high altitude. Parched mountain air causes rapid evaporation of water from the skin and from mucous linings of the respiratory system. Dehydration is aggravated by exercise which directs water to the muscles and increases water loss through perspiration and respiration. Blood plasma volume drops and blood thickens with exertion and with frequent urination, one of the body's adaptations to altitude. The lost fluid and mineral salts **must be replaced.** To fail to do so will invite weakness, lethargy, coordination and orientation problems, headaches, irritability, nausea, and dizziness. Dehydration makes you susceptible to heat exhaustion and heat stroke; it may predispose the newcomer to mountain sickness; it can lead to rapid heartbeat and low blood pressure; in extreme cases it can result in shock. A minor imbalance of the water/body-weight ratio, such as a five-percent unreplenished water loss, can induce symptoms of dehydration.

Dehydration is a treacherous enemy. Thirst is no gauge for measuring fluid depletion; we sense it only after dehydration has begun. Combat this insidious villain by taking small drinks for every 15 to 20 minutes of exercise. **Remember to drink at regular intervals even if you are not thirsty.** Copious clear or light-yellow urine indicates good acclimation and good hydration; infrequent comfort stops and dark urine signal poor adjustment to altitude and/or the need for more liquids. Be conscious of your urine output, and do not delay evacuation.

High-altitude hikers should set off with a generous supply of cool fluid or with the materials needed to purify water available on the trail. Some replacement fluids are better than others. Water is an easy choice. It moves rapidly from stomach to small intestine where it is quickly absorbed.

Rehydration is assured with adequate intake. Water works well for a short hike. But water lacks both taste and the fuel of carbohydrates. The sustained exertion of longer hikes suggests consideration of other fluids.

Fruit juices have taste and fructose, fruit's natural sugar. The fructose concentrations in juices are likely to cause stomach upset during heavy exercise. But juices can be diluted with water and will still deliver energy to supplement your muscle glycogen stores. Sugary carbonated drinks not only tie up water in digestive organs, contributing to dehydration, but can cause uncomfortable bloating. Put sodas on ice in your car to be consumed when you return.

The highly-touted and highly-scrutinized "sports drinks" have advantages for the long-distance hiker. Most contain the simple carbohydrate sugars: glucose, sucrose, fructose; some include electrolytes: potassium, magnesium, chloride, sodium; and others add glucose polymers: maltodextrin, corn-syrup solids, hydrolyzed cornstarch. There is debate among exercise physiologists about the effectiveness of specific carbohydrate concentrations and about the consequent speed of gastric emptying and rate of absorption. But it is generally agreed that an athletic drink with a 5 to 8 percent carbohydrate/glucose polymer content will hydrate adequately and will certainly increase endurance by resupplying the body with fuel. Some athletes choose to dilute the density of these solutions. Personal preference for and tolerance of specific sports drinks seem to be the crucial factors. You will consume more of what you like, and that is the main idea.

Substitutes for heavy, full water bottles are water-purification pumps and unpalatable chemical germicides in tablet form. These alternatives neutralize giardia, an intestinal parasite that lurks in lake and stream water everywhere in the mountains.

Alcohol has no place on the trail as it hastens dehydration, and its effects can be very much like the symptoms of mountain sickness. Visitors who plan to exercise should avoid alcohol altogether until acclimated.

Should you have the misfortune to find yourself short on liquid while still far from trail's end, there are ways to cope. Do not eat. The digestive process requires water. Drink what water you have on the schedule you have established. Do not ration. You cannot alter your water-balance needs.

Slow down to reduce perspiration. Wear a hat. Put on clothing to protect your skin from the sun and drying winds. Breathe through your nose, not your mouth. Do not talk. An old survival axiom states that it is better to ration your sweat than your water.

This leads to one final suggestion. As many trailheads lie miles from the nearest drinking fountain or soda machine, stash liquids in your car prior to your morning departure. A full water bottle will be welcome; a cooler heavy with iced drinks will be wonderful.

Food

The magic word is **carbohydrate**. For those enjoying endurance sports like hiking, nutritionists advise that 70 percent of daily calories consumed should be carbohydrate foods (grains, fruits, vegetables) for sustained energy and for a steady blood sugar level. Some carbohydrates are quickly converted into glucose for immediate use. The remainder are stored as glycogen in the liver and muscles. Strenuous, prolonged exercise will rapidly deplete these stores. An energetic hiker may suffer fatigue, hunger, and even depression from low blood sugar if not refueled with carbohydrate snacks along the way.

So here's a chance to stuff your pack and pockets with fresh and dried fruits, veggie sticks, pretzels, and low-fat granola bars, crackers, and cookies. High-energy, low-fat food bars, called athletic or sports food, have been formulated to deliver the quick punch of simple carbohydrates (sugar) and the sustained power of complex carbohydrates (starches). They also provide an energy release steadier than sugar and faster than starches through a complex carbohydrate derivative known as glucose polymer (the ingredient named maltodextrin, high fructose corn syrup, or hydrolyzed cornstarch). Available at hiking and sports stores, these bars are good company on the longer treks.

Hard candy and chocolate can be integrated into a hiking diet in small amounts. Large concentrated doses of sugar produce energy surges followed by fatigue as blood sugar levels make wild swings. Excess sugar also slows the absorption of water, contributing to dehydration. Fructose, the natural sugar in fruit, is paired with fiber and so is digested more slowly. It is a fine sweet food. Fruit also replaces potassium lost through perspiration.

The other fuels, fat and protein, are slow to digest and more difficult for the body to convert to quick energy. They should each contribute no more than 15 percent of daily caloric intake. Carefully read labels on "energy bars" as fat content ranges from a lean low of 8 percent to an appalling high of 54 percent.

Go easy on fats when you pack for your trail lunch break. Hearty amounts of peanut butter, cheese, or processed meats may induce lethargy just when you need energy. Employ moderation and concentrate on carbohydrates. Fruit-nut breads and bagels, plain or lightly embellished with spreads, are first-rate fodder. Some hikers pack cold baked potatoes, rice cakes, and vegetable sandwiches and salads.

What you eat before and after a hike will also affect how you feel. Start with a dinner of pasta, rice, or potatoes. Add chicken, fish, or lean meat plus vegetables and bread. The combination helps your body both store and replenish glycogen and repairs muscle tissue after exercise. Modest protein intake, animal or vegetable, is essential for repair and muscle-building. Excess protein is stored as fat and converted to fuel only under duress.

A breakfast of whole-grain cereal, muffins, waffles, or pancakes combined with fruit, low-fat milk, or yogurt properly launches you for a vigorous outing. The hiking diet is really just a healthy diet and serves you well whether you are on the trail or in town.

SUSTENANCE

Boots & Gear

"Harmony with land is like harmony with a friend; you cannot cherish his right hand and chop off his left... you cannot love game and hate predators... The land is one organism."

—Aldo Leopold

Boots & Gear

Boots and Socks

COMFORTABLE FEET ARE YOUR BEST TRAIL COMPANIONS. THEY CAN TRANSPORT you to wondrous places. But bruised, blistered feet and stressed, strained ankles can quickly turn enthusiasm into woe. Some mountain paths are gentle slopes paved with dirt. Most, however, exhibit an astonishing variety of terrain. A trail may begin on a level four-wheel-drive road or in a cow pasture; it might proceed across marshes, wet logs, snow, or rushing streams; it often traverses boulderfields and scree; and it may finally conclude with a nearly vertical scramble to a pass or peak.

Running shoes will do for most children and for adults who choose the gentle dirt paths. For all other landscapes we recommend boots with lug soles. They furnish a sturdy base deeply cleft for traction, and they defend against rocks underfoot.

The boot category is a broad one, and although selection should relate to a hiker's intended destinations, comfort and cost are major factors. Backpackers, who haul many pounds for overnight trips, and heavier individuals may prefer the structure and ankle support of heavyweight leather boots. But heavy boots have several disadvantages. Proper fit is essential, as is an extensive "break in" period. Otherwise, blisters may be unavoidable. The weight of such foot gear can also be a burden on longer hikes, hastening the onset of fatigue.

Modern lightweight leather boots provide the support necessary for most long day hikes over uneven terrain and offer reasonable protection from wet brush, bogs, and creeks. The better-quality boots include a waterproof inner layer that "breathes". If one wishes to invest in a single, all-purpose boot, this type is probably the best choice.

The most recent addition to the hiking boot family is a kind of hybrid. Combining the flexibility and near-weightlessness of running shoes with lug soles and above-ankle design, these popular nylon, canvas, or split-suede boots require no painful adjustment period. Early designs granted little defense against water hazards, but some models now offer the protective layer available in leather footgear. Ankle support varies in effectiveness. These boots are a suitable choice for most hikes. If the trail crosses extensive rockfields or snowfields, however, more rugged footgear may be appropriate.

Many water obstacles are obvious from trail guides and maps. Such knowledge is motivation to pack sport sandals or an old pair of sneakers for difficult crossings. Boots and socks stay dry, and the wet shoes can be secreted behind a shrub for the return trip. Extra socks are appreciated after an unexpected slip into a creek or bog. Seasoned hikers tuck a pair into the backpack along with large safety pins for hanging the damp socks out to dry. The pack can double as a moving clothesline. An extra pair of socks can also serve as mittens for cold hands.

Select socks with attention to their fit, cushioning, and "wicking" qualities. Good socks should not trap moisture near your skin. Wool, acrylic, and polypropylene are appropriate fibers. Some hikers place a thin silk or polypropylene sock under a heavy one to guard against chafing and to facilitate wicking. Experiment. Your goal is comfort.

Clothing

The Colorado Rockies are notorious for afternoon thunderstorms that sometimes arrive with little warning. Many hikes also involve major changes in elevation. Before you settle on clothing with fashion appeal, give some thought to the realities of the trail. Imagine shivering past ice-crusted ponds in early morning, brushing against trailside brambles, resting on rocky perches, broiling under a merciless sun, trekking through summer showers, and bucking frigid winds.

Experienced hikers cope with the mountains' diversity by wearing several layers of clothing. Frosty mornings or high elevations may require a windbreaker worn over a fleece pullover or wool sweater. Wool and the new polyester fleece fabrics trap body heat even when wet. This quality can be lifesaving. The tee or tank shirt next to your skin could be your only layer at midday, and you might welcome a hat for protection from the sun. Long sleeves are a wise addition for those who sunburn readily or develop skin irritations from exposure to the intense ultraviolet rays that penetrate high mountain air.

If most of the hike is above treeline where encounters with wind, cold, and hail are common, long pants of tightly-woven fabric are a good idea On a sunny day at lower elevations, comfortable shorts will be enough. (Active leg muscles produce a lot of heat.) Abundant pockets are wonderful for carting small provisions and should be designed into all outdoor garments.

A double-duty, hooded windbreaker/rain jacket is essential for every hike. Shop for a "breathable" fabric such as Gore-tex® to reduce moisture near the skin. Some hikers like to include an additional waterproof poncho voluminous enough to cover a daypack.

 On the longer excursions and those above treelimit, bring pants that are waterproof and windproof. You also need gloves or mittens, extra socks, and a warm, wool hat. A violent storm or an unplanned overnight without adequate clothing can result in hypothermia. This is especially true in the marginal weather of spring and fall when the addition of a down garment is good insurance. Be prepared. The sensations of security and of bodily comfort add tremendously to your enjoyment of the outdoors.

Packs and Pockets

Each time we overtake burdened backpackers inching ponderously toward passes, we are happy to be dayhikers. Even when equipped for every anticipated complication of the journey, we are still lighter on our feet than the overnight crew. Of course, backpackers can retire at the next attractive campsite; dayhikers must make the return trip or complete the loop trail before giving in to fatigue. But with thoughtful planning and all the right stuff in pack and pockets, dayhiking guarantees a satisfying trip into the wilderness.

Packs fall into three general categories: waist/fanny packs, daypacks, and day-and-a-half packs. Hiking enthusiasts may own all three variations; a family or group can get by with a combination of types if its members stick together on the trail.

Your hike's distance, difficulty, and maximum elevation will determine how much you need to carry. Waist packs range from very small to medium in capacity and will suffice for a modest hike, especially at lower elevations. A bulky jacket or shirt can be tied around your middle during warm daytime hours. The common daypack with an outside pouch or two carries enough to take you almost anywhere. The larger day-and-a-half pack, which is designed with a supporting hip belt, is appropriate for the long-haul hiker who is hard-pressed to return by nightfall. Long distances and high elevations make few items optional. Every kind of carrier should have adjustable straps and padding at body contact points.

After tucking away water bottles, food, and extra clothing, add the relevant trail guide. Optional maps include the White River National Forest map and topographical maps based on work by the U.S. Geological Survey. All are available from the U.S. Forest Service office in Aspen and from most hiking stores. The White River map is a useful overview of the area as relationships among roads, trails, mountains, and towns are clearly apparent. Some USGS maps are outdated, reflecting trails now closed or rerouted. Include personal medications and general first aid supplies such as aspirin or ibuprofen, antibiotic ointment, sterile adhesive pads, and packaged cleansing towelettes. Moleskin is positively essential for cushioning blisters. Lip balm, sunscreen, and mosquito repellent should go on every hike. Add a whistle for summoning help and a pocketknife.

More gear is advised for lengthy, less-traveled trails. Learn to use a compass and take it with you. Carry waterproof matches or a disposable lighter, a high-intensity mini-flashlight, tablets or a pump to purify water, a heat-reflective "blanket", and, if traveling alone, a compact emergency flasher.

Many hiking supplies are small and can be stashed in pockets of clothing for easy access. Multipocketed vests made for photojournalists or fishermen might appeal to some trekkers. Ziptop plastic bags are ideal for trail food, can pack out litter, and can be washed and reused. Optional cameras, binoculars, and nature guidebooks add weight but can be nice to have along. And a foam-insulated or drawstring holster keeps water at your waist, encouraging necessary fluid consumption.

BOOTS &
GEAR

The Hikes

"*Climb the mountains and get their good tidings. Nature's peace will flow into you as sunshine flows into trees. The winds will blow their own freshness into you and the storms their energy while cares will drop off like autumn leaves.*"

—John Muir

Trail Summary

	Trail	Aspen to Trailhead (miles)	Hiking Distance * (miles)	Elevation Gain (feet)	High Point (feet)	Hiking Time (hours)
1.	Savage Lakes	52.1	2.8	1170	11044	2-3
2.	American Lake	11.0	6.0	1985	11365	3-5
3.	Cathedral Lake	13.9	5.0	1970	11866	3-5
	Electric Pass		8.8	3610	13500	5-8
4.	Thomas Lakes	28.3	8.2	1600	10240	4-6
5.	Grizzly Lake	16.5	7.0	1950	12520	4-6
6.	Tabor Lake	14.2	6.0	2060	12320	4-6
7.	Hell Roaring	25.6	6.0	2080	12060	4-6
8.	North Fork Lake Creek	24.3	7.0	1580	12460	4-6
9.	Buckskin Pass	10.9	9.0	2860	12460	5-7
10.	Avalanche Pass	60.9	8.0	3040	12100	5-7
11.	Willow Lake Loop	10.9	7.5	3200	12580	5-7
12.	La Plata Peak	29.3	8.0	4175	14336	6-8
13.	Capitol Lake	24.4	12.6	2580	11600	7-9
14.	Pierre Lakes	14.2	14.5	3860	12280	8-11
15.	Snowmass Lake	14.2	17.0	2580	10980	8-11
	Trail Rider Pass		20.6	4000	12420	10-13
16.	East Maroon-Conundrum	7.8	19.8	4240	12900	10-13
17.	Fravert Basin Loop	10.9	23.4	7360	12500	12-15

* round trip distance

Pictorial Overview

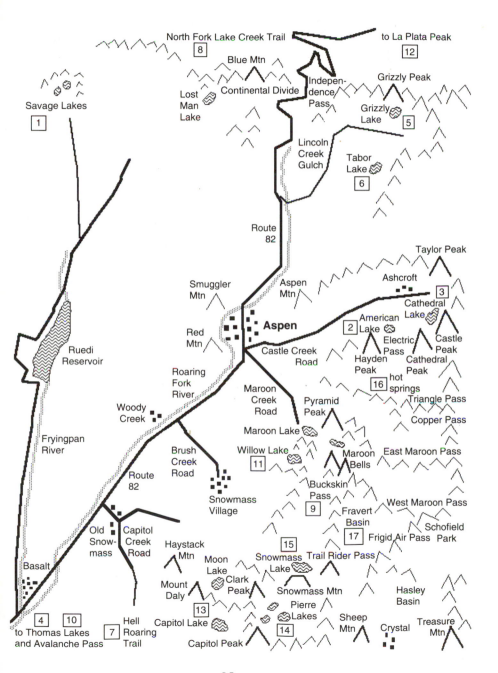

North Fork Lake Creek Trail
8

to La Plata Peak
12

Blue Mtn

Grizzly Peak

Lost Man Lake

Continental Divide

Independence Pass

Grizzly Lake
5

Savage Lakes
1

Lincoln Creek Gulch

Tabor Lake
6

Route 82

Taylor Peak

Smuggler Mtn

Aspen Mtn

Ashcroft

Cathedral Lake
3

Aspen

Red Mtn

American Lake
2

Electric Pass

Castle Peak

Castle Creek Road

Hayden Peak

Cathedral Peak

Ruedi Reservoir

Roaring Fork River

hot springs
16

Triangle Pass

Copper Pass

Woody Creek

Maroon Creek Road

Pyramid Peak

Maroon Lake

East Maroon Pass

Fryingpan River

Brush Creek Road

Willow Lake
11

Maroon Bells

Route 82

Buckskin Pass
9

West Maroon Pass

Snowmass Village

Fravert Basin
17

Schofield Park

Old Snowmass

Capitol Creek Road

Frigid Air Pass

Haystack Mtn

Snowmass Lake
15

Trail Rider Pass

Basalt

Moon Lake

Clark Peak

Mount Daly

Snowmass Mtn

Hasley Basin

4   10
to Thomas Lakes and Avalanche Pass

7   Hell Roaring Trail

13

Capitol Lake

Pierre Lakes

Sheep Mtn

Crystal

Treasure Mtn

14

Capitol Peak

25

Savage Lakes

TRAILHEAD:	52.1 miles from Mill & Main in Aspen
	48.8 miles from rodeo grounds in Snowmass Village
HIKING DISTANCE:	2.8 miles round trip to first lake
	6.2 miles round trip to ridge above third lake
ELEVATION GAIN:	1,170 feet from trailhead to first lake
	2,480 feet from trailhead to ridge above third lake
HIGH POINT:	11,044 feet at first lake
	12,360 feet at ridge above third lake
HIGHLIGHTS:	Scenic drive along Fryingpan River and Ruedi Reservoir
	A short hike with four possible destinations
	Three lakes in grassy, secluded basins
	A jolly stream along the trail

Comments: This is an excellent hike for new arrivals in the high country. The drive is lengthy but lovely. On a bright day sun glints silver off the Fryingpan River; sweet clover waves gold along the roadside; copper bluffs and pinnacles hover high above this deep river canyon; hillsides dressed in multiple greens cradle the giant blue reservoir. The area's elevations are moderate, and the trek itself, though somewhat steep, is short. The lakes are beautiful, and the fishing is good. This hike, with its several worthy stopping points, provides a pleasant way for a new visitor to become acclimated to the mountains.

Aspen to Trailhead: Head west (downvalley) from Aspen on route 82. Drive to the Basalt turn-off on the right side of 82 and follow the road until you reach a small shopping center on the right. Set your odometer, drive down Basalt's main street, and follow the paved road alongside the Fryingpan River out of town (upstream) heading for the Ruedi Reservoir. From Basalt to the Ruedi Dam is 13.7 miles. Continue along the reservoir for another 8.0 miles. There are multiple opportunities to park, stretch your legs, and take in the view high above the water. At the reservoir's top end cross a bridge and then drive through Meredith and Thomasville, country places distinguished by small groupings of buildings and trailers. Farther on, log cabins on the left precede two large, brick, coke ovens standing to the right of the road. At 24.8 miles from the shopping area in Basalt pass the turn-off on your left for the 4-wheel drive road to Eagle (a backcountry route to the Vail area). At 25.6 miles the entrance to the Diamond J Ranch is on your right. The turn-off for the trailhead is a dirt road on the left at 26.0 miles. There is a sign reading "Burnt Mountain" and "North Fork Fryingpan", another for "Elk Wallow Campground", a group of mailboxes, and a third sign for "Mountain Haven Resort Cabins". All signs have arrows pointing left. Bear left here, leaving the main road, but do not take the sharp left turn which goes to the cabins.

The road from this point is unpaved but smooth enough for a comfortable ride in a city car. At 2.1 miles from the pavement a decrepit log cabin sits by a pretty pond; at 2.6 miles a sign on the left points uphill for Burnt Mt. Road and Lime Park; at 4.4 miles the road splits. Keep to the left and drive

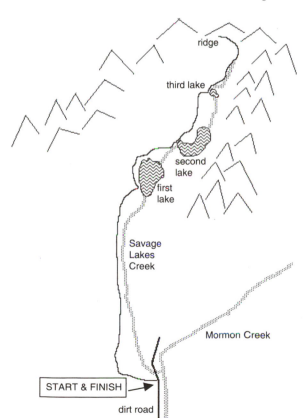

an additional 3.3 miles to the trailhead. It is 7.7 miles from the pavement's end to the trail's beginning. The marked trailhead is on the left side of the road. Parking is across the road on the right. In the last half mile before the trailhead, the road starts to climb noticeably and becomes a bit rougher. The drive from Aspen takes approximately 90 minutes.

Trail Route: A creek marks the hike's beginning, but though it soon vanishes from sight, its sound accompanies the trail as it starts abruptly upward through tall conifers that shade out most sunlight. After a set of switchbacks and about 35 minutes into the hike, the trail straightens and climbs beside this merry creek, the plunging outflow from the lakes above and a feeder of the North Fork of the Fryingpan River. Just before the approach to a large rockfield you enter the Holy Cross Wilderness. Major rock outcroppings appear on the left. In small clearings along the creek on the right, globeflowers, marsh marigolds, and Parry's primroses brighten the forest in July. The trail levels out for a short spell. Huge boulders, dwarfing hikers, lie scattered about. A splashing white waterfall marks the end of the rockfield, and small sidestreams cross the trail. A short steep stretch follows. In early July the track is mucky; it was recently a creek flowing with snowmelt. Just before the first lake, a wooden sign indicates that Carter Lake can be reached by taking a trail to the left. Continue on the main path, fainter now, across a soggy, open meadow where choosing dry footing may be more important than staying on the route. Just beyond the meadow and through some light woods lies the first and largest of the three Savage Lakes. The hike from the trailhead covers about 1.4 miles and usually takes between 50 and 80 minutes, depending on how often you stop to catch your breath.

Sitting in a large bowl, the first lake is ringed by tall narrow conifers. A rocky ridge beyond meets the sky. Even on a perfect blue-sky day, the water appears dark from this vantage point. A noisy waterfall tumbles into the lake. Fish break the surface with regularity. Large boulders invite

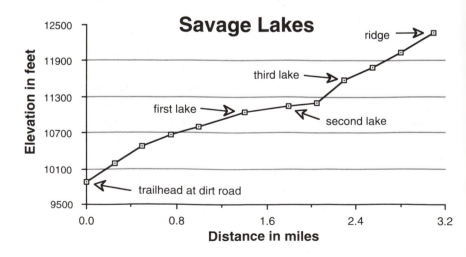

sunbathers and anglers. In July fragile blue Jacob's ladder blooms secretively beneath the trees. The lake's protected setting provides a wonderful sense of solitude, tranquillity, security. This is an excellent place for rest, a snack, and some exploration.

Hikers wishing to find the second Savage Lake should follow a damp trail winding around the left side of the first toward a rock bluff at lake's end. The trail often fades or branches. Fishermen have created many secondary paths. Cross a small inlet stream and move gradually uphill to the right through trees to a spot above the bluff. After about a half-mile of easy walking, the second lake is discovered behind and above the first. Almost as large as the lower one and just as pretty, this lake is slightly less forested at its edge. Fish are abundant.

The third lake is truly alpine, smaller and more shallow than the other two. The search for this hidden lake is only for level-headed adventurers and only for a clear day. The lake is well-secreted above treelimit in a beautiful granite bowl, but it is not served by a trail. The terrain is steep and patterned with rock obstructions and drop-offs. The route begins at the end of a low footpath that edges the left side of the second lake. The path appears to end where a high rock and tree barrier projects into the water. Here, on the path's left, a large boulder, split in two, is topped by conifers. Climb up through the cleft in the rock, bushwhack through the trees ahead, and then choose the spongy, green grassy areas between huge boulders as you move well left of and below a dangerous, vertical rock face. The lake lies above the rock face, but do not attempt to reach it by a direct climb. Continue your steep ascent over grass until you are as high as the bluff's top edge and then proceed to the right into the bowl. A tarn is a clue that you are close. Continue to the right into a lovely scene where a lacy waterfall and high snowy ridge lie beyond the lake's water. A brook babbles through flowers and grasses, and nearby waterfall sounds locate the lake's outflow over the cliff behind you. The first two lakes are easily seen from this cliff, the top of the rock face.

Though the distance from the second lake is not great, this excursion may take additional time if backtracking and exploration are required. Check the sky for dark clouds as you evaluate your progress. On your return trip remember to swing wide to the right around the cliffs. Stick with grassy footing until reaching the trees through which the lake below is visible.

The ridge above the third lake is 0.8 miles away and requires another 30 to 50 minutes of climbing. The elevation gain is an additional 780 feet. The best approach begins near the waterfall that feeds the lake. If you reach this ridgetop, you will have an excellent view of all three lakes and their geographical relationship. In addition, you will have a breathtaking view of the Holy Cross Wilderness area lying on the opposite side of the ridge. For the ambitious hiker, this spectacular vista of several dozen major peaks is a well-earned reward.

American Lake and Beyond

TRAILHEAD:	11.0 miles from Mill & Main in Aspen
	17.1 miles from rodeo grounds in Snowmass Village
HIKING DISTANCE:	6.0 miles round trip to American Lake
	7.4 miles round trip to alpine basin above lake
ELEVATION GAIN:	1,985 feet to American Lake
	2,700 feet to alpine basin above lake
HIGH POINT:	11,365 feet at American Lake
	12,080 feet at basin above lake
HIGHLIGHTS:	Several pretty meadows along the trail
	A fishing lake in a sheltered setting
	Panoramic vista from flowery basin above the lake

Comments: This is a hike of easy to moderate difficulty with a trailhead only 25 minutes from downtown Aspen. One can visit the lake and return in half a day. The trail's first mile climbs steadily through bright aspen woods and is most comfortable in early morning when the air is cool and the sun is low.

Aspen to Trailhead: Head west (downvalley) from Aspen on route 82. At 1.3 miles from Mill and Main in Aspen turn left at a traffic light and chapel onto Maroon Creek Road. Take an immediate left onto Castle Creek Road. Proceed for 9.8 miles up a beautiful valley until you see Elk Mountain Lodge to your left. On your immediate right is the parking area for American Lake trail. If you reach the ghost town of Ashcroft, you have driven about one mile too far.

Trail Route: The first 1.3 miles of the dirt trail is a relentless climb via a series of long switchbacks through aspen woods spotted with columbine and blue flax, paintbrush and yarrow. The sun is intense on this part of the trail as airy aspens provide little shade. The steep ascent is easiest in the early day when ridges and peaks block direct rays. Across a wide gulch from the trail, a slope receives less sunshine and is clad in dark conifers. The pleasant sound of a creek accompanies the route's beginning, but soon it vanishes. After about 50 minutes of steady climbing, the trail enters a cool spruce forest. At this point in the hike you are at an altitude of 10,500 feet and have gained over half the elevation to the lake.

Here the path rises less sharply and has welcome level stretches. A few minutes after entering the evergreens, the trail crosses an immense, sunny, double meadow. Its sloping expanse is bisected by a stand of conifers where, in the shade, lavender-blue Jacob's ladder blooms in profusion. The trail re-enters conifers and climbs a ridge at 10,900 feet. A short descent

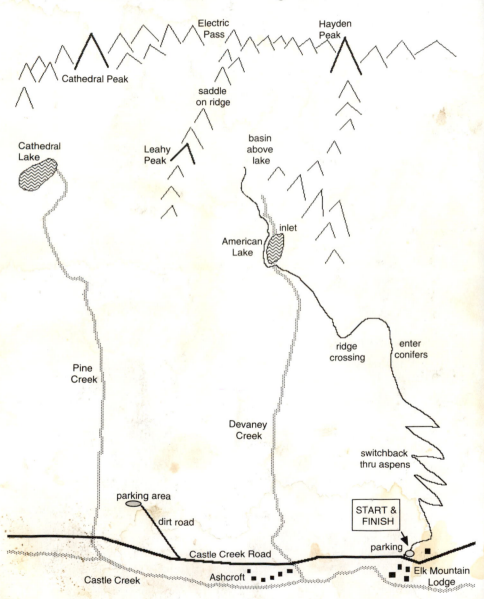

takes you briefly through aspen woods, and after another 10 minutes, into a second large meadow. The first hikers of the morning may spot deer. In the distance sits a bowl surrounded by high ridges. American Lake, still hidden, is nestled in that bowl.

A few minutes of hiking brings you to a third meadow distinguished by a huge rockfield at its upper end. Pikas may register high-pitched complaints at your disturbing presence. Ahead at another rockfield the view opens out revealing mountain peaks and Devaney Creek dashing down an opposite ridge. The rockslide drops abruptly left of the trail. Raspberry bushes flourish in this barren spot and offer sweet fruit in late August. The path leads through trees and, suddenly, delivers you at the lake. The hike from trailhead to lakeside usually takes about two hours. *took us about 2½ hrs.*

American Lake is not impressively large nor particularly deep, but the site is picturesque and an enjoyable locale for lunch. It often attracts other hikers. Some drop lines for the small fish cruising the water close to shore. Bold gray jays beg for food scraps. Alpine anemones and globeflowers bloom by water's edge.

If the sky is clear and the day is young, you may wish to cross the outlet, birthplace of Devaney Creek, to tread a footpath along the lake's left side. Opposite the outlet, a small stream empties into the lake. A lightly-traveled trail ascends beside the stream. If you are ready for a stiff climb, follow the

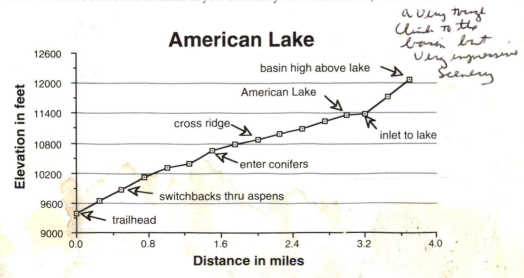

a very tough climb to the basin but very impressive scenery

American Lake

basin high above lake

American Lake

cross ridge

inlet to lake

enter conifers

switchbacks thru aspens

trailhead

water up through a spongy meadow of grasses, marsh marigolds, and rocks. As the flow diminishes, cairns—carefully piled rocks—mark the way. As you pursue the cairns up the steep hillside, you gain an excellent view of the lake. Alpine wildflowers thrive here, and marmots, ptarmigan, and deer are in residence.

Continue upward, bearing left of a notch distinguished by a rocky butte on its right and evergreens on its left. Avoiding the loose rock of the notch, the cairns lead left of the evergreens and toward a mammoth upper basin. Stop occasionally to appreciate the scene behind you. An early glimpse of snowy peaks matures into an awesome mountain tableau. Nearby the remnant of an old road scars an opposite hillside.

The upper basin is enclosed by Hayden Peak on the right at 13,561 feet and a lofty ridge to the summit's left. You may spy hikers above you on this ridge which crests a precipitous talus slope. They are following the trail from Cathedral Lake to Electric Pass and are only a few minutes from their goal. At 13,500 feet, Electric Pass is the highest named pass in Colorado. The basin's floor is richly carpeted with grasses and tundra flowers. In the distance are the jumbled pinnacles of the Collegiate and Gore ranges. It takes some effort to reach this destination, but the alpine splendor is an adequate reward.

Cathedral Lake and Electric Pass

TRAILHEAD:	13.9 miles from Mill & Main in Aspen
	20.0 miles from rodeo grounds in Snowmass Village
HIKING DISTANCE:	5.0 miles round trip to Cathedral Lake
	8.8 miles round trip (direct) to Electric Pass
ELEVATION GAIN:	1,970 feet to Cathedral Lake
	3,610 feet to Electric Pass
HIGH POINT:	11,866 feet at Cathedral Lake
	13,500 feet at Electric Pass
HIGHLIGHTS:	Picturesque mountain lake at the foot of Cathedral Peak
	Bountiful alpine wildflowers above lake
	Great variety in terrain
	Splendid view of Elk Mountains from Electric Pass

Comments: This is a hike of moderate difficulty with a trailhead 35 minutes from downtown Aspen. One can visit the lake and return in half a day. The trail is fairly steep and is climbed most comfortably in the cool morning. The lake offers fishing for trout. Though the climb to Electric Pass above the lake is arduous, the wildflowers and vistas are well-worth the effort. Electric Pass is the highest named pass in Colorado.

Aspen to Trailhead: Head west (downvalley) from Aspen on route 82. At 1.3 miles from Mill and Main in Aspen turn left at a traffic light and a chapel onto Maroon Creek Road. Take an immediate left onto Castle Creek Road. Drive for 12.0 miles up a beautiful valley past the Elk Mountain Lodge and the ghost town of Ashcroft. Beyond Ashcroft look for a dirt road on your right. Follow the dirt road for 0.7 miles to reach a parking area.

Trail Route: As with many nearby trails, the climb begins on soft dirt through aspen woods. Pine Creek is audible as it tumbles down from Cathedral Lake. Twenty minutes from the trailhead stands a sign on the left stating "No Camping Here" in what was obviously once a campsite. Just beyond on the right is the wilderness boundary sign. As the route begins to parallel the creek, the grade becomes steeper and the footing more uneven. Here, in mid-August, delicate harebells mix with trailside grasses, and the first gentians bloom. After traveling through a clearing with a rockfall on your right and a conifer-topped ridge towering above, you enter a mixed forest of aspens and evergreens. This transition demonstrates elevation change. Soon the trembling aspens will be left behind.

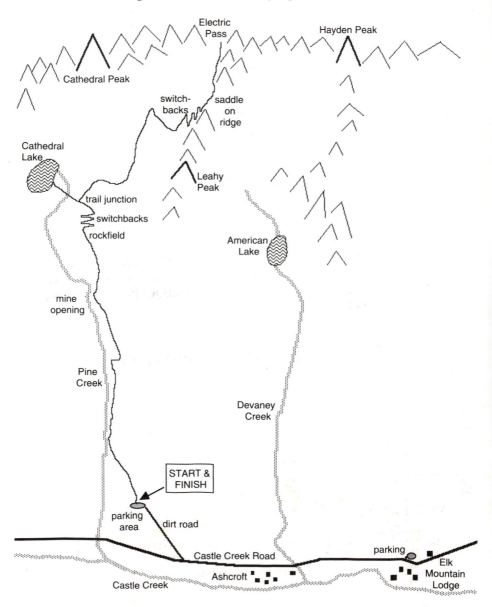

After about 50 minutes of climbing, the trees thin out for a wider survey of the scenery below and the road to Taylor Pass across Castle Creek valley. The path shadows the creek and overlooks a series of cascades that plunge down a precipitous gulch. A few minutes beyond is the rush of a stair-stepped waterfall where Pine Creek plummets into a rough-walled crevasse. Approximately an hour into the hike you traverse a small rockfield with some low shrubs and a few scuffy conifers. From here you can see a neatly-cut mine entrance in the red wall across the creek. A stand of conifers grows above the mine, and loose stones are everywhere in the forbidding spot.

Beyond the rockfield, the trail travels along the creek for about a half-mile with little elevation gain. About 70 minutes after leaving the trailhead, you stand in a lovely, open spot with a large, wet, willow-filled meadow stretching out below. This flat marsh may be the remnants of an old beaver pond, now filled with silt. A sign near an old trail turnoff reads "Closed for Re-vegetation". Talus lies to the left, and a pointed peak stands between it and a rounded mountain to the right. The trail ascends again and bisects a rockfall area dominated by red buttes. About 90 minutes into the journey is another boulderfield, red-hued and extensive. The final approach to the lake's bowl waits directly ahead. The trail climbs via a series of short, sharp switchbacks. Pausing in your ascent, you can spot mine openings chiseled into the vertical rock face opposite.

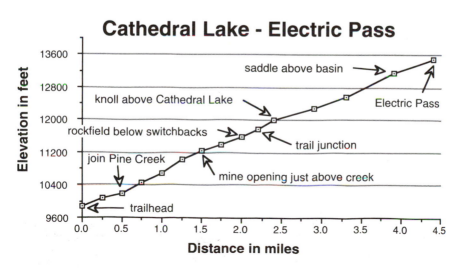

Cathedral Lake - Electric Pass

At the top of the switchbacks, proceed left where you encounter a wooden sign at a split in the trail. To the left is a short walk, about 0.3 miles, to Cathedral Lake. To the right is a two-mile, vigorous hike to Electric Pass. The trail to the lake drops briefly, crosses a small stream, and then forges uphill gradually. If the weather is friendly, it is easy to settle in a pleasant spot near the water for lunch. But if an afternoon storm threatens, you should not linger. The lake is above treelimit with no nearby shelter. Lightning is a serious threat in any exposed area.

If the sky is blue or dotted by a few puffy clouds, and if you feel vigorous, you may wish to bypass the lake's shore and climb directly toward Electric Pass. If the sky is overcast, it is wise to refrain from this journey. Electric Pass is extremely dangerous in a storm. It is aptly named.

The dirt trail is well-marked and sets forth by leading you toward jagged spires constituting the right ridge of Cathedral Peak. The ridge extends to Electric Pass and connects to Mt. Hayden high above American Lake. After a short distance the trail bifurcates with the lower path taking hikers on another route to the lake. From here and beyond, Cathedral Lake is a glistening vision, reflecting sky and mountain. As you turn from the lake view to begin long switchbacks up to a saddle, a dip in the ridgetop, look for an orange stain on the maroon slope to your right, evidence of an iron miner's dig. Two additional iron digs lie ahead opposite a loose rock pile to the trail's left.

The path gains elevation gradually but relentlessly as it switchbacks up the side of a ridge beneath Leahy Peak, a high point of 13,322 feet. You climb through a vast, scenic, high meadow of willows, grasses, and wildflowers. This is an excellent place to carry a field guide to alpine flowers as the rich variety multiplies with minor changes in elevation. Look for alpine sunflower, an oversize, fuzzy, yellow composite that consistently faces east. The journey from the lake to the saddle on the ridge takes 60 to 90 minutes of steady hiking. At 13,000 feet, less oxygen is available, and breathing is laborious. The saddle falls away to your right into a valley that houses American Lake. The lake is hidden, but Hayden Peak at left presides over the landscape.

Electric Pass is still 20 to 25 minutes away. Head west, to the left, and follow the cairns (rock piles) marking the route to the pass. After ascending along the ridge, the trail skirts left of Electric Pass Peak and moves horizontally across a scree slope, an area of small, loose rocks. Sometimes the path is indistinct. After a quarter-mile of careful stepping, you reach the goal. From a vantage point of 13,500 feet you have awesome views. To the south nearby Cathedral Peak dominates the landscape. To the west rise Pyramid Peak and the Maroon Bells. In the distance is Snowmass Mountain, Hagerman Peak, and behind them, Capitol Peak. The climb from trailhead to pass takes 3 to 4 hours.

The main trail terminates at Electric Pass which overlooks a deep valley, home to Conundrum Creek and the popular Conundrum hot springs. The Conundrum side of the pass is a treacherous, vertical place of loose rock. The trail traversing this dangerous slope is no longer maintained and is not a recommended route to the valley. Taking the hiker to Electric Pass Peak at 13,635 feet is a short, lightly-marked side trail that travels up a ridge to the north. A splendid vision of the entire wilderness area justifies the extra exertion.

Thomas Lakes

TRAILHEAD:	28.3 miles from Mill & Main in Aspen
	25.0 miles from rodeo grounds in Snowmass Village
HIKING DISTANCE:	4.1 miles round trip to first large lake
ELEVATION GAIN:	1600 feet
HIGH POINT:	10,240 feet
HIGHLIGHTS:	Beautiful drive with tremendous views of Mount Sopris
	Two pretty lakes and two ponds sheltered below treeline

Comments: This easy to moderate hike is found on the northernmost boundary of the Maroon Bells-Snowmass Wilderness. With modest elevations and mileage, this excursion is appropriate for newcomers to the mountains. Although the hike's beginning is not particularly interesting, the lake area is lovely and an excellent place to explore, fish, or relax. Because the location is "downvalley" where summer temperatures can be high, start your hike early to reach the cool region of the lakes before midday. Thomas Lakes is a popular spot for campers who plan to assault majestic Mount Sopris, the twin-peaked giant that reigns over the lower Roaring Fork Valley.

Aspen to Trailhead: Drive west (downvalley) on route 82 past the turnoffs for Snowmass Village and old Snowmass. Continue beyond the first exit for Basalt, and at 19.6 miles from Mill and Main in Aspen, turn left from 82 at a sign for Sopris Creek Road and the tiny community of Emma. Make an immediate left turn onto East Sopris Creek Road, drive a short distance, and make a right turn onto West Sopris Creek Road near a row of mailboxes. Pass a small group of houses and quickly find yourself in cattle, horse, and sagebrush country. Handsome ranches spot the valley, and the roadside is awash with golden woolly mullein, rabbitbrush, and sweet clover. Monumental Mount Sopris is directly ahead; both of its granite peaks soar to 12,953 feet. A high shoulder forms the mountain's left flank, and a small hump is connected at right.

At the second of two cattle guards, 25.7 miles from Aspen, the road becomes gravel. Just 0.3 mile beyond, turn right at a sign for Dinkle Lake. The road winds high above the valley and seems to move away from

Mount Sopris before it twists again toward the mountain. In another 0.4 of a mile, turn left onto road 311. (It is here that another route via Carbondale meets this road to the trailhead. See below.) Road 311 is dirt, and while not in wonderful condition, can be cautiously negotiated in a highway car. After 1.9 miles on road 311 you reach a parking area and a brown sign on the right reading "West Sopris Creek 2, Thomas Lakes 3, Hay Park 3". Dinkle Lake is nearby below the parking lot.

An alternate route to the trailhead for travelers from Glenwood Springs involves turning south onto route 133 at Carbondale. Follow 133 for about three miles and look carefully for Prince Creek Road (road 111) on the left. Drive 6.2 miles on road 111 to the junction with road 311.

Trail Route: The hike begins on an old four-wheel-drive road through a mixed forest of aspen, fir, and lodgepole pine. The broad track heads right for a half-mile and then switchbacks left, toward the east, for another half-mile as it climbs a hill. Horses also use this lower trail, and they leave obstacles and flies for the hiker. Occasional sandy patches mix with rocky footing. About 30 minutes from the start, an opening in the trees offers a view of Dinkle Lake and a peek at the left shoulder of Mount Sopris. The trail continues through the forest, rounds a ridge, and takes an abrupt right to Thomas Lakes.

A few minutes beyond the lookout

Mount Sopris

second lake

first lake

pond

Prince Creek

pasture

trailhead

START & FINISH

Dinkle Lake

parking

dirt road

point is a large meadow and a sign reading "Closed for Revegetation". Logs across the old trail emphasize its closure. A sign for Thomas Lakes directs hikers to the left on a circuitous route which loops around the grassy, flowery hillside—a hillside that serves as a pasture for cattle. Purple lupine blooms here in early summer; in August western coneflowers stand tall, their dark cylindrical heads bereft of ray flowers.

Beyond the meadow is a short steep section of trail which levels out before moving into an aspen grove. You can still recognize the route as an old road by the double tracks through the grass. In the woods grow mosses, mushrooms, and wild strawberries. Flowering here and all along the route is northern yellow paintbrush—pale, often branching, and taller than its more alpine cousin, the solitary western yellow paintbrush. This spot can be reached after about 60 to 90 minutes of steady hiking.

The next open space is ringed by trees and blossoming with fragrant bedstraw, pussytoes, and yarrow. Horse and cow manure have been left behind. A bit more climbing takes you to a field that, in August, is entirely lavender with aspen daisies. Dark conifers stand beyond, and Sopris can be seen through the trees. The path moves in and out of evergreens.

At about 3.7 miles there is a big pond to the right of the trail. It is blue-green in color, shallow, and encircled by trees. A marshy area of tall grasses is

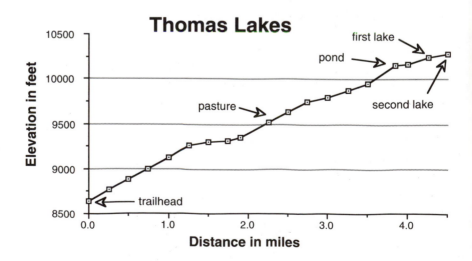

42

opposite. While it may be tempting to stop here, hikers are encouraged to step toward more beautiful locales ahead.

The track is rough, interrupted by large rocks, as it conducts you through willows. There is the sound of running water as a creek links the pond with the first of the Thomas Lakes, snug in a rocky bowl at right. The path bifurcates here. A wilderness boundary sign stands next to a post bearing four messages including "Thomas Lakes" and "Main Trail" (with an arrow pointing right). Steer right where you encounter side trails that pass through a few trees to water's edge. A naturally air-conditioned spot is found at the lake's far end where an incoming stream drops from a higher, small pond.

To discover the second Thomas Lake, continue on the rock-strewn main trail. The shoulder of Sopris is directly ahead. Two small signs with triangular symbols indicate campsites. The lake area is flat and has good tree cover for campers. Beyond the campsite signs, the trail again divides. The left fork guides hikers to the final lake and starts climbers on their trek to the big mountain ahead. In August gentians border the wide path. Fireweed, another late-bloomer, is here as well.

The second lake is soon in sight, and within minutes the remains of a log cabin stand between you and the shoreline at left. The shallow water has a periphery of aspens, conifers, and loose rocks. The trail edges the lake and then climbs a bluff at its south end. This vantage point makes a good conclusion to the hike.

It is here above the water that the trail to the Sopris summit begins. Bearing to the right, this route has been improved recently by volunteers who cut switchbacks and built steps to create an alternative to the nearly-vertical, old approach. The twin peaks soar almost 2,800 feet above the lakes—a hearty climb. The native Utes called Sopris "Big Mountain with Snow on Top".

Grizzly Lake

TRAILHEAD:	16.5 miles from Mill & Main in Aspen
	25.2 miles from rodeo grounds in Snowmass Village
HIKING DISTANCE:	7.0 miles round trip
ELEVATION GAIN:	1,950 feet
HIGH POINT:	12,520 feet at Grizzly Lake
HIGHLIGHTS:	Open flowery meadows after short uphill in woods
	The majesty of the Continental Divide
	The music of sprightly Grizzly Creek
	The cutthroat trout of Grizzly Lake

Comments: This journey is easy to moderate and quickly takes the dayhiker to subalpine meadows where mountain vistas combine with wildflowers and gentle terrain. Though the start and finish are steep, the path is primarily dirt and does not require heavy boots. Because of the exposure above treelimit, however, attention to weather conditions is important, and a warm clothing layer may be needed at the lake.

Aspen to Trailhead: Drive east from Aspen on route 82 heading for Independence Pass. At 10.0 miles from Mill and Main in Aspen turn right on a dirt road entering Lincoln Creek Gulch. This road is rough and requires slow, careful driving with a city car. Proceed downhill for 0.5 miles and pass the entrance of Lincoln Gulch Campground. Stay left at the fork. At 3.2 miles from route 82 you see the New York Creek trailhead; at 4.2 miles you pass the turnoff for the trail to Tabor Lake. Beyond the Tabor trailhead the lodgepole pines thin out, and the view opens up. At Grizzly Reservoir, bear left where a sign says "Portal Campground". A wood fence is on the right with the reservoir below. A trailhead sign on the road's right side is opposite the wooden sign-in box present at most trail beginnings. A small parking area is on the left just beyond the signs. You are 16.5 miles from Mill and Main and 6.5 miles from route 82. In a four-wheel-drive vehicle the trip from Aspen takes about 45 minutes.

Trail Route: Just after starting uphill, you reach a Collegiate Peaks Wilderness boundary sign on the right. The trail climbs sharply through spruce woods into patches of blinding early morning sun and places where shadows are deep. Grizzly Creek burbles along far below on the right. After about one-half mile and 15 to 20 minutes of exertion, you arrive at the first of many cheery meadows that carpet a large valley. The views improve with this level, open space of grasses and flowers. A rounded, bald mountain borders the meadow on the right; a craggy ridge rises on the left; a high wall of stone lies in the distance ahead. Mixed among the grasses are white yarrow and the white puffs of American bistort, blue harebells and northern yellow paintbrush.

Three times after emerging from the initial wooded slope, stands of conifers divide one meadow from another. The steady presence of low willows signals a nourishing dampness where Grizzly Creek flows. At one point the trail bifurcates. A tree lies across the lower creekside path. This is an indication that it is closed or is not the main route. The footpath remains well-defined and easy on feet. Towering lousewort, a July bloomer, is one of the larger plants that appears often on the first half of this trail. The Continental Divide, with its many snowfields and forbidding character, barricades the end of the valley. The north face of Grizzly Peak is its dominant feature.

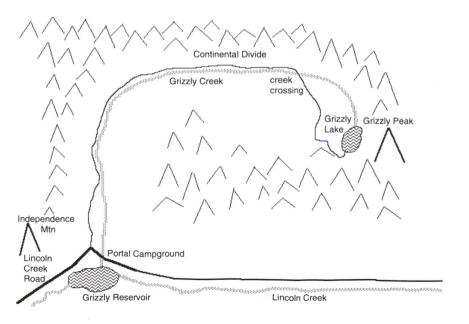

An hour into the hike, at about the two-mile point, you pass a small, roofless log cabin on your left. This marks the final conifer grove. Beyond stretches an ample, upper valley with a sensational, multicolored, wildflower display. Here too, just beyond the cabin, the trail descends slightly to cross Grizzly Creek. Water music now flows to the path's left as you weave upward through a wild garden of gentians, purple fringe, and death camus. A small sidestream cuts the path, and a pretty waterfall cascades down the valley's right facade. The trail begins to mount more noticeably after the water crossings. The wreckage of a small plane rests in the valley to the left, and several mine digs are on the right.

A bend in the trail reveals a narrow waterfall tumbling from the jagged ridge ahead. Marmots often frolic here and beyond. Rosy paintbrush dazzles with its brilliant color and its enormous numbers. After about 90 minutes of steady walking from the trailhead, the valley narrows and the path becomes very abrupt as it climbs a cliff above the creek. A cold wind may catch you in this higher, more exposed place. It is here that the trail bends sharply to the right toward the southwest and gives a fine view of Grizzly Peak. Straight ahead, nearer and lower than the peak, is a prominent rough butte with a rounded top. Grizzly Lake is secreted behind this rocky outcropping. Follow the trail to the right, moving away from the creek to enter a level marshy area with several tarns. Another turn in the trail and a short ascent toward the ridge carry you to a damp upper valley. The trail may be faint in this and all wet areas. Always check for cairns and look ahead for drier slopes where routes are better defined. At this point the

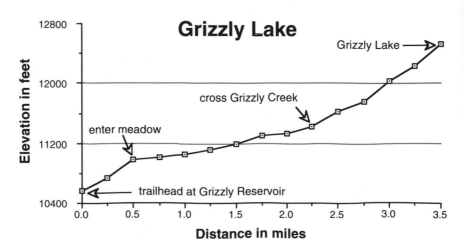

46

trail seems to steer away from the goal as it ascends to the right, but it soon doubles back, climbing the face of the ridge and heading straight for the bowl that cradles the lake. This depression sits to the right of the round butte and behind a smooth green shelf. A high ridge on the far right holds a snowbank in midsummer.

Beyond the boggy area is a serious uphill. It crosses a rockfall area softened by fragrant Colorado columbine. From above, the marsh scene is more watery than it appeared earlier. The trail turns to the right at the top of this steep ascent and conducts hikers across level tundra to the northeast end of the lake. The alpine fishing lake is contained in a deep basin below craggy, unfriendly Grizzly Peak. Brown and red streaks on the mountain's slope give the water a dark reflection. The circumference of the lake is a vertical composition of loose rock. Green places are confined to the approach to the lake and the far left side beyond a slope into which a narrow trail is cut. A climb to the knoll above the lake will improve views and add generously to sightings of tundra wildflowers.

The trip to the lake takes between two and three hours. Assume the longer time if you are new to the mountains. Deduct a quarter of the ascent time for the return.

Tabor Lake

TRAILHEAD:	14.2 miles from Mill & Main in Aspen
	22.9 miles from rodeo grounds in Snowmass Village
HIKING DISTANCE:	6.0 miles round trip
ELEVATION GAIN:	2,060 feet
HIGH POINT:	12,320 feet at Tabor Lake
HIGHLIGHTS:	Trail parallels a lively creek
	Two impressive waterfalls en route
	Long alpine meadow exuberant with wildflowers
	Icy lake hidden far above treeline

Comments: The trail mounts steeply at the start for about 0.6 miles, climbs very gradually for the next 1.8 miles, and then makes a stiff ascent to the lake for the final 0.6 miles. Because the footpath disappears for a stretch, observational skills are important. Early in July the trail frequently traverses snowbeds, sidestreams, and marshy areas. There are two major creek crossings where an old pair of sneakers may be helpful.

Aspen to Trailhead: Drive east from Aspen on route 82 heading for Independence Pass. Exactly 10.0 miles from Mill and Main in Aspen turn right on a dirt road entering Lincoln Creek Gulch. This road is rough and requires slow, careful driving if you have a city car. Proceed downhill for 0.5 miles and pass the entrance to Lincoln Gulch Campground, staying left at the fork. At 3.2 miles from route 82, note a sign on your right for the New York Trail. Continue for another mile (4.2 miles from route 82) until you see the entrance drive on your right leading to the Tabor Lake trailhead. There is enough space to park five or six cars. If you are in a 4-wheel-drive vehicle, the trip from Aspen takes about 40 minutes. If not, add an extra 20 minutes.

Trail Route: The trek begins at 10,260 feet. From the trailhead you see a forested area and a bald, rounded mountaintop across Lincoln Creek. Partway up the wooded slope is a horizontal scar. This is a road running parallel to the New York Collection Canal which carries water from the Rockies' western slope through a tunnel to Colorado's eastern slope cities. The Tabor Creek trail crosses this canal.

Depart the trailhead and face the immediate challenge of fording wide
Lincoln Creek. Move upstream 30 or 40 yards to locate two large fallen trees
that make the crossing easier. Next, head downstream a short distance,
navigating around some wet spots, until you see a path heading into the
woods. Cut by a small sidestream at its start, the rocky trail climbs sharply
for 0.2 miles through a fragrant forest of mixed conifers (spruce, pine, and
fir) until it intersects the canal road. Cross the canal on a sturdy wooden
bridge and note a sign for Tabor Creek trail. The path continues uphill
through conifers and soon joins boisterous Tabor Creek below on the right,
your companion for the next two miles. As the trees thin out, several
varieties of paintbrush provide color. About 25 minutes from the parking
lot, you must cross Tabor creek via two end-to-end log spans. Usually some
long sticks lie nearby to help you balance as you cross.

On the creek's other side the trail ascends steeply for a short time and then
arrives at a spacious meadow. Here the trees give way to a grand vista of
high ridges sheltering a verdant broad valley. The route continues along
the valley's right-hand (south) side. Tabor Creek runs briskly through a gulch in the valley's center and nourishes willows, brookcress, and chimingbells. The trail continues to climb gradually through meadows rich with grasses and wildflowers. In late July this special place resembles an oriental carpet as flowers of every hue ornament the ground. Blue columbine and rosy paintbrush form stunning displays. Although snow patches will slow

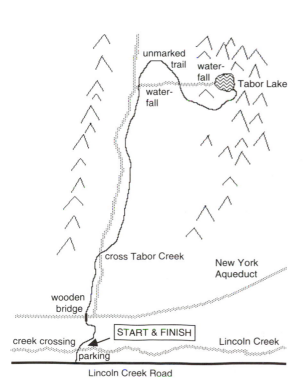

49

progress in early July, the pathway here is mostly dirt, and hikers can move along quickly. Look for shiny, golden, oversize alpine buttercups next to melting snowbeds. If colored by the protective red pigments of resident algal plant cells, the snow will have a watermelon-pink cast. Ahead, at the upper end of the valley, stands a craggy ridge forming part of the Continental Divide. The high point to the left of the saddle is Truro Peak.

As you approach the valley's end, small groves of conifers mark your progress. Soon the valley floor below slopes sharply, and Tabor Creek can be seen descending in a whitewater cascade. Beyond this point, a small stream flows over the trail. Look down for brilliant magenta Parry's primroses. Look up to the right to discover a graceful lacy waterfall that becomes the stream at your feet. It is outflow from Tabor Lake. As the path continues up the valley, it gains elevation and becomes quite faint in grassy places. Begin to look for cairns, arrangements of piled rocks, to find the way.

The cairns signal the need to depart the valley corridor and to climb south toward the ridge where Tabor Lake is secreted. There is no regular trail over this rock-strewn, grassy hillside. With luck, you will discover cairns that designate the route to the lake. As you reach each cairn, scan carefully for the next. Check the skyline ahead for rough jagged pinnacles that form a dip in the ridge. One thin projection resembles a long finger. Move toward this spot. As you crest a hill, your view includes a dramatic cataract left of the pinnacles. Like a moving curtain, the water drops in front of two giant

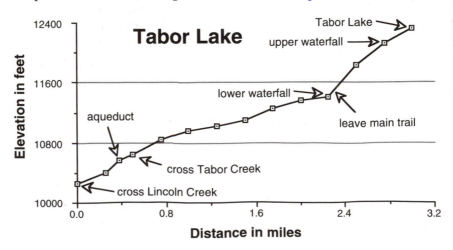

hollows in the rock wall backdrop. Boulders lie below you to your left; a sodden, green area skirts the bottom of the boulderfield; and the Tabor Lake trail reappears beyond this marsh to the waterfall's right. The lake sits directly above the waterfall.

Pick your way over the rock-covered slope or bypass it by dropping down to the damp pretty meadow. This low spot makes music with its variety of water sounds. Move toward the waterfall's right to pick up the distinct dirt trail that ascends steeply up and to the left. The lake is very close.

Given its location, Tabor Lake is larger than you might expect. It also appears deep. There are no trees here. Even "krummholz", the stunted trees of high mountains, cannot survive this environment. But despite its elevation of 12,300 feet, the lake contains fish. Ice floats near shore in early July, and snow often persists at water's edge through the summer. The journey from trailhead to lake usually takes about two and a half hours.

Hell Roaring Trail

TRAILHEAD:	25.6 miles from Mill & Main in Aspen
	22.3 miles from rodeo grounds in Snowmass Village
HIKING DISTANCE:	6.0 miles round trip from trailhead to unnamed pass
	8.5 miles round trip from Capitol Lake trail parking area
ELEVATION GAIN:	2,080 feet from trailhead to pass
	2,640 feet from Capitol Lake trail parking area to pass
HIGH POINT:	12,060 feet at pass
HIGHLIGHTS:	Photogenic, layered red rock formations
	Views into deep lush valleys on both sides of trail
	More wildlife than hikers
	Optional sidetrips to Williams and Hardscrabble Lakes

Comments: The stunning vista at the hike's start overlooks Capitol Creek valley and Capitol Peak. This is a prelude to the theme of the trip's upper reaches. The trail twines up a narrow ridge between two plunging valleys before it begins a final climb to a pass, a climb often complicated by snowfields. There are spots along this trail which suggest its colorful name: blood-thirsty mosquitoes ambush the unprepared in the first mile; rain produces a quagmire of slippery red mud; and steep segments test commitment. But the hike is not a long one, and the visual rewards of this journey make it a place worthy of return trips. The trailhead, a mile and a quarter above the Capitol Lake trail parking area, is hard to reach without a four-wheel-drive vehicle.

Aspen to Trailhead: Proceed west from Aspen on route 82. Drive past the Snowmass Village turnoff at Brush Creek Road and continue 8.5 miles downvalley to the turnoff for old Snowmass. Turn left from 82, drive for 1.8 miles, and then turn right at the intersection of Snowmass Creek Road and Capitol Creek Road. Follow Capitol Creek Road, passing a left turnoff for St. Benedict Monastery. Head directly toward a rocky, snow-spotted expanse that stretches from Mt. Sopris near Carbondale to Capitol Peak. The goal of this hike is a pass on top of that rocky expanse. The road deteriorates to dirt at 6.5 miles from route 82. A mile beyond is a picturesque old barn on the right. Farther along is a parking area for those who haul horse trailers. At about nine miles from 82 the road becomes very rough. This place is a mile from the parking area for the Capitol Lake hike and 2.2 miles from the Hell Roaring trailhead. Newer cars should probably be parked here. A four-wheel-drive vehicle, a truck, or an old city car can likely be taken as far as the Capitol Lake trailhead. Beyond that spot a nimble 4WD vehicle is desirable. The road is steep and heavily rutted for the final 1.2 miles and 600 feet of elevation gain. A large grass-encircled pond and a green metal gate mark the start of Hell Roaring trail.

Trail Route: A verdant yawning valley, traversed by a twisting creek and beaver ponds, spreads below the cliff edge where the trail begins. Vast stands of pale aspen contrast with stately conifers attired in dark forest hues. Dominating everything is august Capitol Peak standing in the distance, its vertical ridges accentuated by snow. Mt. Daly, to the left, is Capitol's companion. This view can be savored again from lookout points on the route ahead.

The earth and rock path is maroon-red and leads into a conifer forest, pleasantly aromatic but often inhabited by mosquitoes and flies. A

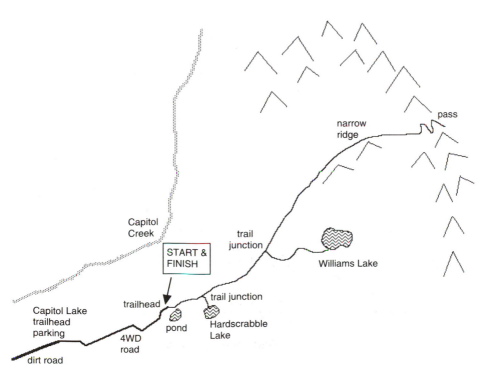

wilderness sign stands just inside the woods. Tree roots crisscross the trail. A ten-minute walk brings you to a turnoff on the right to small Hardscrabble Lake, a short stroll from the main route. Twenty-five minutes beyond, also to the right, is the trail for Williams Lake. Larger than Hardscrabble, Williams at 10,815 feet elevation is encircled by trees and is found about a mile from this turnoff point. Signs for both lake trails have recently disappeared.

Beyond the second sidetrail, the path steepens sharply as it ascends the spine of a ridge. As the trail gains elevation, flies and mosquitoes are left behind. A series of switchbacks and about 15 minutes of steady uphill brings you to the first viewpoint from a cliff edge at the path's left. The Capitol Lake trail is apparent in the valley below as it crosses an avalanche area between two stands of trees. Much of the Roaring Fork Valley opens behind you, and beyond it the distant Gore Range is visible. Continue upward through the trees, and in a level place where the trail seems to bifurcate, bear right. About 30 minutes from the first lookout spot you near the right edge of this narrow ridge and can peer down at a forested valley and Williams Lake. Mount Sopris commands the skyline to the northwest.

As you advance, note a small, green meadow tucked among trees far below on the trail's left. Elk sometimes gather there in summer. Beyond some maroon rock piles and about 25 minutes after viewing Williams Lake, the trail reaches a flat area below the unnamed pass that is the hike's

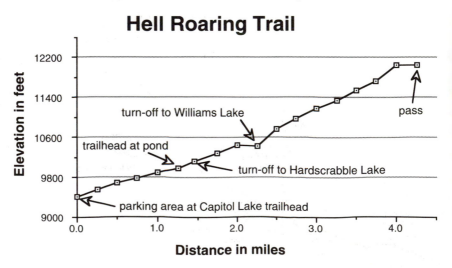

destination. This moist flowery spot lies at 11,450 feet. Trees are replaced here by glacier lilies, globeflowers, and marsh marigolds. A tarn supplies water to wildlife.

A red dirt trail switchbacks up the slope ahead for the final 600 feet of elevation gain. Snow buttercups flourish beside melting white patches. Sky pilots and alplilies bloom among low grasses. In July snowfields may slow progress toward the nearby goal.

The pass area is broad and beautiful with its tundra flowers, red rocks, and sweeping prospect. A grassy hollow tucked among the rocks offers sunny seclusion and protection from wind. A carpet of blue alpine forget-me-nots keeps company with rockjasmine, moss campion, dwarf clover, and alpine sandwort. The scenery glimpsed during the climb is spread out in all its magnificence. The ridge on which you stand connects neighboring Mount Sopris with Capitol Peak to the southeast.

And over the pass stretches a new view and a little-traveled part of the wilderness. The Hell Roaring Trail continues for many miles as it descends along Hell Roaring Creek and lower Avalanche Creek to Avalanche Campground and eventually to route 133 in the Crystal River Valley. The trail is, additionally, part of a loop backpack trip that follows Hell Roaring Creek downhill, then ascends along upper Avalanche Creek, crosses a pass next to Capitol Peak and above Capitol Lake, and returns via Capitol Creek to the trailhead 1.2 miles short of the Hell Roaring start.

North Fork Lake Creek Trail

TRAILHEAD:	24.3 miles from Mill & Main in Aspen
	33.0 miles from rodeo grounds in Snowmass Village
HIKING DISTANCE:	8.0 miles round trip without 4WD vehicle
	7.0 miles round trip with high-clearance 4WD vehicle
ELEVATION GAIN:	1,660 feet without 4WD vehicle
	1,580 feet with high-clearance 4WD vehicle
HIGH POINT:	Pass on Continental Divide at 12,460 feet
HIGHLIGHTS:	Gentle flowery trail through high mountain valley
	A sparkling creek and an unnamed, alpine fishing lake
	Views from the Continental Divide

Comments: This easy to moderate excursion begins with a scenic drive on the spectacular Independence Pass road to the east side of the Continental Divide. Much of the hike is a very gradual uphill with the final 600 feet requiring real exertion. It is a trail best traversed after mid-July as creek crossings are difficult earlier and marshy areas are more extensive. Extra socks or waterproof boots are recommended. Wildflowers are abundant, and the entire hike has open beautiful vistas. Carry a warm clothing layer as the pass may be windy and cold, and always survey the sky when above treelimit.

Aspen to Trailhead: Drive east from Aspen on route 82 to Independence Pass. At 19.8 miles from Mill and Main you reach the pass on the Continental Divide where there are observation areas, an elevation sign, and parking. Continue on route 82 as it drops via long switchbacks. At the third and final hairpin turn, 4.5 miles from the Independence Pass sign, drive left onto a dirt road. The area is lush with the water from the North Fork of Lake Creek. Fishermen are often in evidence. Park at this junction or proceed to another spot a short distance further along. An agile, high-clearance, four-wheel-drive vehicle can negotiate the rutted road for about one-half mile. There is no trailhead sign until the hike is underway.

Trail Route: If you begin at the switchback on route 82, hike north along the dirt road, which is fringed by low willows. Conifers and mammoth boulders are scattered in the grassy terrain. The Independence Pass road is up to your left. The North Fork of Lake Creek is at right, and beyond it is a mining road. One-half mile from route 82, the trail road climbs a knoll to its conclusion. From the knoll you can spot tailings from the Champion Mine. To continue the hike bear left at a tall blue spruce onto a footpath.

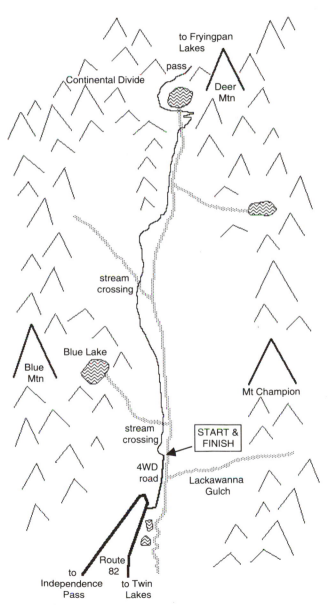

to Fryingpan Lakes

pass

Continental Divide

Deer Mtn

stream crossing

Blue Lake

Blue Mtn

Mt Champion

stream crossing

START & FINISH

4WD road

Lackawanna Gulch

Route 82

to Independence Pass

to Twin Lakes

The trail heads north, makes a short ascent, and levels out in a mountain meadow. A slanted peak stands in the distance ahead. A ten-minute walk along the path brings you to the trail register and a small wilderness sign. Nothing identifies the trail by name. Just ahead is the crossing of outflow from Blue Lake, hidden above in an alpine basin at 12,495 feet. Small unsteady logs serve as a bridge. As you proceed gradually uphill, many sidestreams cut the dirt path. The main creek is at right in this broad U-shaped valley. Conifers are spotted about, but the route is not wooded. Nodding groundsel and several varieties of gentian bloom here in August. Slopes at the near left are dressed in green. Towering ridges to the right lift above treeline. As the trail winds toward the enclosed end of the valley, the scene ahead expands to reveal a smooth snowy ridge, part of the Continental Divide. At the valley's upper end the path swings left to skirt a marshy area near the creek.

The major stream-crossing of the hike is 2.5 miles from route 82. It may be challenging in July and could require considerable bushwhacking until a suitable spot is found. The water feeds the North Fork of Lake Creek which remains on your right. Begin to look for cairns after the crossing as the trail is sometimes indistinct. Look back as you walk and note the rocky outcropping topped by conifers that marks the ford. It can be seen at some distance and will aid your return should the path be faint.

Beyond the creek the grade increases as the trail continues toward the valley's upper end. A big basin with high walls is the valley's western boundary. After winding around large rocks and bushes, the trail bears right, or east, to mount a low ridge into the drainage beyond. With elevation gain the tops of peaks at Independence Pass emerge behind you, but the pass you seek remains out of sight. A short steep climb over some boulders at the ridge takes you through a notch into the secondary valley that has been partially visible for most of the hike. The trail, well-worn here, turns left and edges a slope above the North Fork. The creek originates

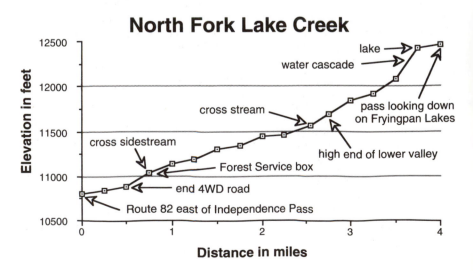

at the unnamed lake above. As the route moves closer to the water, plant growth in the wet level places often sabotages the trail. Cairns help you navigate. Look for them as they conduct you directly toward a round-top mountain and over the creek on the valley floor. Ahead, where the route begins its final and very stiff uphill, the path is conspicuous.

The stream from the lake above creates a slender sinuous waterfall left of the switchbacks leading to the pass. At one scenic point after the first switchback, it splashes through layered red rocks bordered by white and yellow flowers. After the second switchback the trail makes a few small turns and traverses the waterfall's upper end where snowbanks may remain in summer. From here the prospect of grand peaks includes prominent Blue Mountain at 13,711 feet to the southwest on the Divide. This landmark is designated as Twining Peak on the topographic map. The picture below is of a multitude of rivulets snaking through the secondary valley.

A short walk brings you to a lake sheltered in a low area right of the trail. Continue along its left shore over grass and between rocks and move slightly uphill to the pass ahead. The new vista is of the Fryingpan Lakes tucked into a narrow valley in the Hunter Fryingpan Wilderness. In the distance stand the mountains of the Holy Cross Wilderness. A tarn nestles below the pass. Deer Mountain at 13,761 feet forms the right wall of the pass. Beyond it, toward the Fryingpan Lakes, rises Mount Oklahoma at 13,845 feet. Both peaks are part of the Continental Divide.

The lake's pretty, grassy shoreline and its resident fish make it a pleasant stopping place on a sunny day.

Buckskin Pass

TRAILHEAD:	10.9 miles from Mill & Main in Aspen
	17.0 miles from rodeo grounds in Snowmass Village
HIKING DISTANCE:	9.0 miles round trip
ELEVATION GAIN:	2,860 feet
HIGH POINT:	12,460 feet at pass
HIGHLIGHTS:	Proximity to three fourteeners
	Stunning view of Snowmass Lake from pass
	Two lakes and a turbulent creek en route
	A distinct, well-marked trail

Comments: The journey to Buckskin Pass is one of the most popular in the Maroon Bells-Snowmass Wilderness. It is scenic from parking lot to pass and gives the hiker an up-close-and-personal feeling for some of the tallest, most dramatic mountains in Colorado. Snow remains below the pass into summer, and one minor stream crossing adds interest.

Aspen to Trailhead: Drive west (downvalley) from Aspen on route 82. Make a left turn onto Maroon Creek Road at the chapel and traffic light 1.3 miles from Mill and Main. Bear right immediately at the fork and continue for 9.6 miles to the Maroon Lake campground where a narrow road winds up to a parking area. Remember that Maroon Creek Road is closed to private vehicular traffic after 8:30 a.m.

Trail Route: Several footpaths wend through a meadow from the parking lot to Maroon Lake. A nature trail and beaver lodge make this a favorite destination for tourists ferried here by bus. Keep to the far right side of the lake and walk southwest through light aspens. A large sign warning of the danger of climbing "The Deadly Bells" stands at the water's far end. Continue to bear right on the main trail as it mounts by way of some short switchbacks. Abundant rocks and tree roots cause uneven footing. Excellent viewpoints along the trail here and beyond afford photographers opportunities for permanent memories of Maroon Lake, the Maroon Bells, and Pyramid Peak.

The trail enters a substantial rocky basin and marches directly toward the Bells. Furry sunbathing marmots and small bustling pikas are residents here and are likely to broadcast your arrival with shrill whistles and squeaks. Low raspberry bushes, alpine wallflowers, groundsels, and scarce red columbines grow among the rocks. A slight downhill anticipates a trail junction just short of Crater Lake, which is about 1.6 miles from the trip's start. The West Maroon Trail leads hikers alongside the lake on its way to West Maroon Pass. Continue by taking the right fork for the Maroon-Snowmass Trail to Buckskin Pass.

Crater Lake remains in sight as you move upward through aspens for about half a mile. The track then continues uphill, makes a few short switchbacks, and moves along a ravine carved by rambunctious Minnehaha Creek. More gentle switchbacks through spruce woods bring you, after another 0.8 miles, to a minor stream crossing. In late June, in places just freed from snow, yellow glacier lilies carpet the earth like dandelions while budding, deep red king's crown prepares for its summer show. Pyramid Peak crowds the landscape behind you and North Maroon Peak is the intimate neighbor

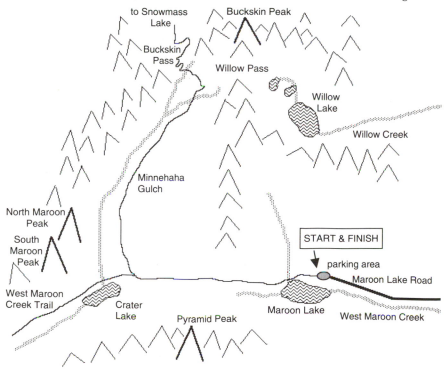

61

on your left. An unnamed peak tops the right wall of the gulch. There is an enormity to nature's architecture here; human insignificance is palpable.

About 20 minutes after the water crossing, the trail turns to reveal Buckskin Pass, a low spot on the horizon to the northwest. Soon you enter an expansive meadow with a "no camping" sign and then encounter, after crossing the meadow, a trail junction. The sign here directs hikers right to Willow Pass and Willow Lake and left to Buckskin Pass. Take the left fork and ascend via switchbacks for the hike's final mile and 700 feet of elevation gain. In early summer, snow may force detours as you approach your destination. Use caution and be willing to abandon the effort if the snowpack creates a total blockade.

Buckskin Pass is an end worthy of the exertion required to attain it. Here is a 360-degree spectacle. This is Colorado at its best. West of the pass with a summit of 14,092 feet is white Snowmass Mountain standing sentinel over its deep lake. Just left of the mountain's high point lie Hagerman Peak and Snowmass Peak, together one massive stone fortress. Adjacent to the southeast, at a dip in the ridge, sits Trail Rider Pass. Descending to the deep valley below, a trail carries hikers from Buckskin Pass to Snowmass Lake and its mighty guardians. Capitol Peak, another of the Elk Mountain's famous fourteeners, rises to the right rear of Snowmass Mountain. A harsh ridge of peaks runs south of Buckskin to North Maroon Peak, the much-photographed fourteener and symbol of the Aspen high country; the ridge north of the pass tops out at 13,370 foot Buckskin Peak; to the southeast is Pyramid Peak, yet another mountain over 14,000 feet.

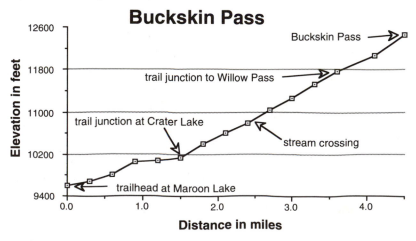

Avalanche Pass

TRAILHEAD:	60.9 miles from Mill & Main in Aspen
	57.6 miles from rodeo grounds in Snowmass Village
HIKING DISTANCE:	8.0 miles round trip from trailhead
	9.6 miles round trip from turn-off for Crystal
ELEVATION GAIN:	3,040 feet
HIGH POINT:	12,100 feet at Avalanche Pass
HIGHLIGHTS:	Crystal River canyon south of Carbondale
	Multiple waterfalls and bountiful wildflowers
	Solitude and a real sense of wilderness
	Breathtaking panorama from pass

Comments: This pleasant excursion is worth the 90-minute drive. Despite its extraordinary beauty, the moderately difficult trail is not heavily traveled. The landscape has variety and countless flowers. The many stream crossings dictate extra socks or waterproof boots. Rise early to reach the goal. A four-wheel-drive vehicle is useful for the final stretch of road (though this distance of 0.8 miles can be covered on foot).

Aspen to Trailhead: Head west (downvalley) from Aspen on route 82. Drive past Brush Creek Road (road to Snowmass Village). Continue on 82 past the signs for the small communities of old Snowmass, Basalt, and El Jebel. After about 30 minutes turn left onto route 133 at Carbondale. A traffic light marks this major intersection. Snake through the deep, slender Crystal River canyon on 133. Sun does not illuminate this crevasse in the early morning. Fisherman seek trout in the river's turbulence. Chunks of discarded marble are incongruous riverbank ornaments. You pass the main entrance to historic Redstone, an old coal-mining community, at 17.5 miles from route 82. Coke ovens border the roadside. Drive 5.1 miles further along route 133 and make the left turn for Marble, home of the Yule marble quarry. Here the road quality deteriorates. After a little more than five miles a sign locates Marble's town limits. The main street makes several turns as it continues east to Beaver Lake, a mile past the sign. Edge the north side of the lake and ascend on a dirt road for 1.5 miles. At a junction take the left fork for Lead King Basin (and avoid the precipitous, downhill road to the ghost town of Crystal). It is here that four-wheel-drive is useful. Lost

Trail Creek flows right of the road; a turnoff for the Colorado Outward Bound School is to the left as you advance. The trailhead is 0.8 miles from the junction, just before the North Fork of Lost Trail Creek crosses the road. Park on the right under trees near the creek.

Trail Route: A National Forest Wilderness sign and a trail registry box mark the hike's start. Begin the trip with a climb uphill through airy woods of aspens and conifers. The trail is made narrow by high grasses and flowers. Cow parsnip, tall and stately, seems to be everywhere. The forest's soft dirt surface is easy on the feet. The North Fork of Lost Trail Creek is right of the path and is the first water obstacle 15 to 20 minutes after setting forth. At a fork in the trail, bear right and drop down to the creek for the new, relatively easy crossing on sturdy logs. (The old ford is straight ahead about 70 yards and offers a good chance for wet feet.) Beyond the log "bridge" ascend on the fresh track to the creek's right. Heavy undergrowth makes the path obscure in places, but it soon connects with the older, better-defined route.

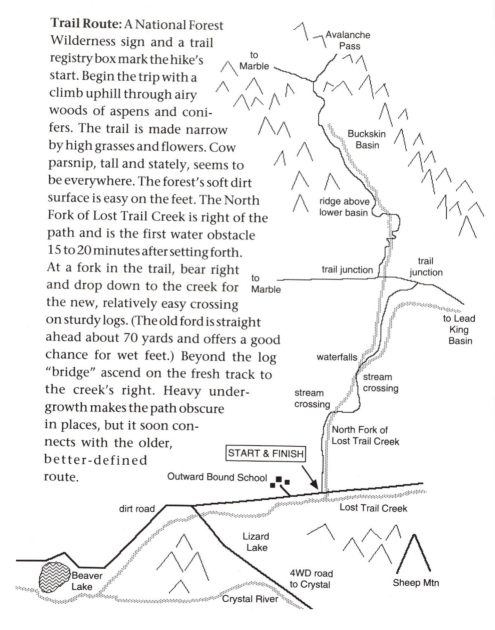

Avalanche Pass

to Marble

Buckskin Basin

ridge above lower basin

to Marble

trail junction

trail junction

to Lead King Basin

waterfalls

stream crossing

stream crossing

North Fork of Lost Trail Creek

START & FINISH

Outward Bound School

dirt road

Lost Trail Creek

Lizard Lake

Beaver Lake

4WD road to Crystal

Sheep Mtn

Crystal River

After about an hour you emerge from the trees onto more level ground. The vista includes a lush valley, lofty ridges, and many flowers, including scarlet gilia/fairy trumpet and blue Colorado columbine. Lying among grasses below the trail is what appears to be an old steam-driven engine, a remnant of mining days. Approach the creek again where it spreads wide over flat layered rocks. The trail makes a 180-degree turn to lead hikers downhill to the water. After crossing at this pleasant spot, with the creek now on the right, hike through brilliant blue flax. Within a few minutes, the trail passes along a narrow ridge between two lively streams. A pair of white waterfalls soon comes into view on the right. A few paces along are two larger cataracts—one on each side of the ridge. The left cascade dashes over stair-stepped rocks. Beautiful.

About 90 minutes into the trip you pass through a stand of conifers near the valley's upper end. Here you meet a trail traveling perpendicular to the one on which you hike. The right fork takes hikers to Lead King Basin. Choose the left fork and move into a sodden meadow at the base of a rockslide. This is the bottom of Buckskin Basin where wildflowers grow waist-high. Sheep Mountain governs the lower valley behind you. On all other sides you are enclosed by ridges and by the flowers through which you wade: chimingbells/mertensia, delphinium, and statuesque spikes of Case's fitweed with its surprising lilac scent. About 30 yards after a stream-crossing at the end of this luxuriant meadow, scout for another trail junction—a junction poorly marked and easily missed. Take a right at a

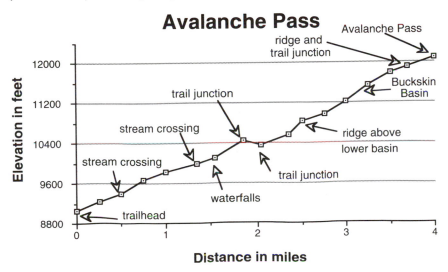

65

small cairn just off the trail on your right. (The path leading straight ahead makes a long march to Marble.) Another cairn about 50 feet up the hillside confirms your heading.

The trail now climbs steeply up a rockslide along a stream. Make a fourth crossing where the water pours sharply down over stones. The trail is rough, vague, mostly rocks. Water flows on both sides of the uphill route. After a fifth crossing, there is a show of orange sneezeweed, an awkward bright composite. The trail then moves up a ridge, providing an aerial view of the basin you just departed. Continue along the stream as you aim directly for a lovely, bowl-shaped meadow in a valley perpendicular to the one below. This is upper Buckskin Basin. In July king's crown blooms with bravado in the flat wetness as you continue to step over running water. It is hard to distinguish flooded trail from narrow stream in this marshiness. Rosy paintbrush and avens carpet the ground, and brookcress blooms in the stream. In fact, everything flourishes here. Move ahead into a large, level, beautiful meadow. Color is everywhere.

Continue your ascent to alpine tundra. The approach to the pass is a steep, worn, dirt trail. A false no-name pass with its resident snowfield must be negotiated on the way to the real thing. Once over the false pass, do not continue straight ahead on the trail. Make a sharp right turn for the gradual, one-third mile climb to conspicuous Avalanche Pass. At the top you enjoy an uncommon perspective of the Maroon Bells-Snowmass Wilderness. The West Fork of Avalanche Creek curls like a ribbon in the valley far, far below. Mount Richey is nearest the pass—a stone presence with a gray-apricot hue. Beyond it stand, left to right, Mount Daly, Capitol Peak, a ridge of Capitol, the top of Clark Peak, and, farther in the distance, Snowmass Mountain and adjoining Hagerman Peak. Tiny tundra flowers seem too fragile for this wild place, this place of giants. Look close to the earth for dotted saxifrage, alpine sandwort, moss campion, pygmy bitter-root/lewisia, rockjasmine, and whiproot clover.

Avalanche Pass trail has physical challenge, powerful images, and precious, delicate beauty. It offers all this to the few who make the journey. The pleasant return trip usually takes one-third less time than the ascent.

Willow Lake Loop

TRAILHEAD:	10.9 miles from Mill & Main in Aspen
	17.0 miles from rodeo grounds in Snowmass Village
HIKING DISTANCE:	7.5 miles for full loop trip
ELEVATION GAIN:	2,420 feet to Willow Lake
	3,200 feet to Willow Pass
HIGH POINT:	12,580 feet at Willow Pass
HIGHLIGHTS:	A private valley high above Maroon Lake
	Large alpine basin surrounding Willow Lake
	Grand views of wilderness from Willow Pass

Comments: This moderate to difficult loop hike includes two stiff uphills and approaches Willow Lake by a rarely-used trail. It returns by a conventional route over Willow Pass. As the trip's high-altitude point occurs after the lake visit, pay heed to the weather before lingering at water's edge. Two hundred feet of elevation gain is lost in descending a ridge to Willow Lake.

Aspen to Trailhead: Head west (downvalley) from Aspen on route 82. Turn left at the chapel and traffic light onto Maroon Creek Road at 1.3 miles from Mill and Main. Stay to the right at the fork. Drive 9.6 miles to the Maroon Lake campground and follow a narrow road as it winds up to the parking area on the right. Remember that Maroon Creek Road is closed to private vehicular traffic after 8:30 a.m.

Trail Route: Begin at the parking area's far end just below the restroom building. Cross a small stream immediately and follow the trail downhill through tall grasses and flowers. About twenty yards after a second small water crossing, look for a white rock to the trail's left and for an indistinct, narrow path opposite the rock to the right. The path leaves the main trail and leads uphill toward a waterfall. The first goal is a stand of aspens visible on the ridgetop.

The steep hillside meadow is a riot of color as wildflowers thrive in the sunshine and moisture. An absence of switchbacks makes a challenge of this 800-foot ascent. Aspens partway up the slope provide welcome handholds. A spring emerges from bare earth and flows left of the trail. This initial climb takes 30 to 45 minutes.

On gaining the ridge you acquire a new perspective. Maroon Lake gleams far below and Pyramid Peak, distinctive with its horizontal grooves, rises to the south. The scene ahead is of meadows carpeting a long valley closed at its end by a steeple-topped, red mountain. Deer browse here in the early morning. The path is faint and meandering, nearly overgrown from disuse. Keep to the right to avoid a gulch. As you begin a climb through low evergreens, the rocky terrain obliterates the trail. Search out cairns (rockpile markers) to guide you. Some distance from valley's end a large and final cairn sits at the base of a huge rockslide. Turn uphill to the right, and ascend over loose rock to the ridge high above. The footing is unstable, and the climbing is difficult.

Your toil is rewarded at the top by the sight of Willow Lake directly below and the presence of a well-defined, diagonal path down the slope. Willow

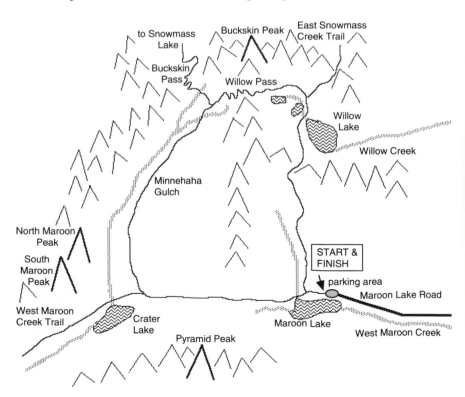

Lake resides in a spacious basin holding neighboring ponds and tarns. Trails lead from the basin's floor northeast down Willow Creek—a route now closed by private land; northwest over a pass to East Snowmass Creek; and southwest to Willow Pass and the route back to Maroon Lake. The distance from the parking area to this alpine, treeless spot is about 1.5 miles.

In departing, walk between the main lake and the small ponds to its west to intersect the main trail traversing the center of the valley. Once on this trail, head west across the flat damp basin toward Willow Pass. Within a few minutes you reach a fork. A sign directs hikers left toward Willow Pass, a mile away. The trail to the right heads for East Snowmass trail over a pass visible on the ridge to the northwest. From this point until hike's end there is no ambiguity about the route. Willow Pass is evident, and the gentle grade makes easy work of the 800-foot elevation gain. Alplily, moss campion, and purple-leaf groundsel are three of the many tundra flowers that survive in this rugged place.

The hike's high point, Willow Pass, delivers views of mountains and valleys to the north and south. North Maroon Peak dominates the southern skyline. To its left is the West Maroon Creek valley leading to West Maroon Pass. Minnehaha Gulch below is home to a sinuous stream and the trail that takes hikers the 2.7 miles to Crater Lake, another marker on this loop

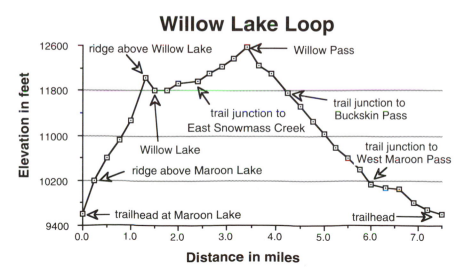

69

trip. Look about for marmots who frequent this lofty place. The descent from the pass is precipitous and includes switchbacks as it drops into a spectacular basin with high walls of loose rock. A small stream crossing is followed by a series of switchbacks leading into Minnehaha Gulch. Tumbling water on your left, nature's wild garden, and a new look at Pyramid Peak add visual excitement. Alpine avens and moisture-loving flowers—king's crown, alpine anemone, and marsh marigold—all prosper here.

At the top of the gulch and about 30 minutes after departing the pass, you encounter a sign at a trail junction. The pathway to the right goes uphill on the popular Maroon-Snowmass trail to Buckskin Pass. The left fork pilots hikers downhill toward Crater Lake. Elevation here is 11,760 feet. Another 20 minutes of descent brings you to spruce woods and the ford of Minnehaha Creek. This stream stays on your right as you proceed to Crater Lake.

The route from here to Crater and Maroon Lakes covers well-traveled territory. Several sidetrails lead to campsites. As conifers give way to aspens, you are close to Crater Lake, which can be glimpsed through the trees on the right. Access to its shoreline comes at a junction for West Maroon Trail and Maroon-Snowmass Trail. Maroon Lake and the loop's beginning lie to the left about 1.6 miles through a level open rockfield and a descent through trees. This final lake is also to the trail's right, and the parking area is just across the meadow on the water's far side.

La Plata Peak

TRAILHEAD:	29.3 miles from Mill & Main in Aspen
	38.0 miles from rodeo grounds in Snowmass Village
HIKING DISTANCE:	8.0 miles round-trip
ELEVATION GAIN:	4,175 feet
HIGH POINT:	14,336 feet at summit of La Plata Peak
HIGHLIGHTS:	Fifth-highest mountain in Colorado
	Sweeping perspective from the state's roof-top
	Invigorating aerobic experience

Comments: The fourteeners in Aspen's immediate neighborhood are not good choices for novice climbers. Castle, North and South Maroon, and Pyramid peaks are notorious for insecure, "rotten" rock. Capitol and Snowmass provide more stable footing but require experienced climbers. In contrast to the Elk Mountains, those in the nearby Collegiate Range are slightly taller, more solid, and comfortably rounded on top. Of these fourteeners, La Plata Peak has the trailhead closest to Aspen. La Plata is particularly enjoyable because the access trail is scenic, the ascent involves rock-climbing without dangerous drop-offs, and the panorama from the summit is magnificent. Additionally, the ascent route along a major ridge facilitates keeping a wary eye on weather conditions. Start the climb in the early morning to gain the peak by noon. And always depart any summit or exposed ridge before thunderheads gather.

Aspen to Trailhead: From Aspen follow route 82 as it twists upvalley toward Independence Pass. It is 19.8 miles from Mill and Main to the elevation sign at the pass. Set your trip odometer to 0.0 at the sign and continue east toward Twin Lakes, descending the pass via switchbacks. When your trip odometer approaches 9.2 miles, look right for a sign marking a dirt road, South Fork Lake Creek Road. Turn here, cross the bridge spanning North Fork Lake Creek, and drive 0.3 miles. Look for a spot to pull off the road and park. There is no designated parking area.

Trail Route: The first quarter-mile of the trail has been rerouted recently. The trailblazers thoughtfully identified the new course with orange tape, and if these markers remain, you will easily start off in the proper direction.

The path begins left of the dirt road and heads east through a grove of trees toward South Fork Lake Creek, about a quarter-mile away. The main trail is beyond this flow. In 1992 a well-constructed bridge spanned the creek. If the bridge is still intact, use it. Otherwise, you must wade. It is not an easy ford.

Once across the creek, climb the bank and scout for a trail parallel to the water. Go left on this trail, away from La Plata Peak. In a few minutes the path turns right and leads toward a nearby drainage. It continues through light woods and passes over a small stream en route. Soon you reach La Plata Gulch, access corridor to the mountain. The trail bends right again and accompanies the stream up the gulch. You have come about one mile from the trailhead. The route along the gulch is a bit steep but clearly defined. Climb through forest for another mile. The trail then enters a pretty valley with gentle, more open terrain.

Walk up the valley for about a half-mile, scanning left for a trail that ascends a rocky area. Along this rough uphill the track is indistinct in places. Look ahead with regularity to stay on the correct heading. At this point the objective is to scramble to the ridgetop on the valley's left side. The difficulty is that the valley floor is at 11,200 feet while the shoulder of the mountain rises to 12,720 feet. You need to gain about 1500 feet of

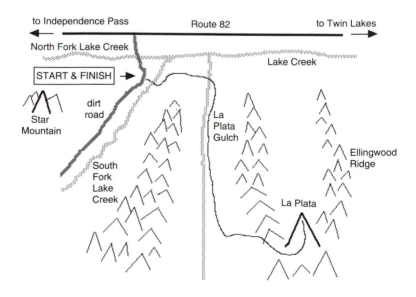

elevation in a half-mile of trail. If you have not climbed a mountain before, this section of trail provides an excellent introduction.

Once you have attained the ridge, take a right. The formal trail disappears, but this is not a problem. The route to the summit is obvious. The peak is now about a mile distant and 1600 feet above you. Move along the ridge toward the highest point on the skyline. Several patches of big boulders require clambering on all fours or hopping from boulder to boulder. A large snowfield usually rests on the left of the upper ridge. To avoid this obstacle stay right, keeping your boots dry and avoiding a slide. As you reach the highest portion of the ridge, La Plata's summit comes into view on your left. A great pile of rocks denotes the top. There is an official elevation marker placed there by the U.S. Geological Survey and a receptacle containing a pencil and a list of the names and addresses of earlier visitors to the peak. Take time to add your name to the record.

From the crown of La Plata you have an astonishing vista. Directly to the north is Mount Elbert, the tallest mountain in Colorado. Just beyond Elbert is Mount Massive. This gigantic mountain, standing as guardian over Leadville, Colorado, has five peaks over fourteen-thousand feet. "Massive", indeed.

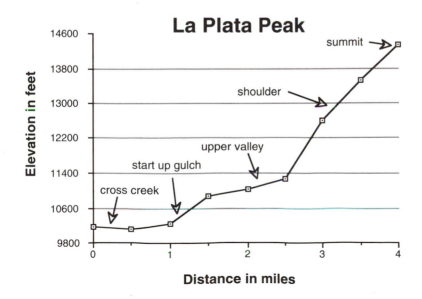

Looking south along the Collegiate Range you see, from left to right, Oxford, Belford, Missouri, and Huron—all over fourteen-thousand feet. To the west, the tallest mountain in the foreground is Grizzly Peak, and in the distance stand Snowmass and Capitol. On a clear day look far to the north and slightly to the east to see Longs Peak in Rocky Mountain National Park. The climb up La Plata is rigorous, but the reward at the top more than compensates for the effort expended.

Close by the summit rears a ridge approaching from the north. Long, narrow, and jagged, it is inviting only to climbers seeking an extraordinarily difficult challenge. Ellingwood Ridge is named for an experienced technical climber who, in 1921, was the first to reach the summit via this route. Albert Ellingwood was awarded a Rhodes Scholarship in 1910, earned a law degree from Oxford, and was Assistant Dean at Northwestern University when he died in 1934. In 1960 a three-man party attempted a winter ascent along Ellingwood Ridge. They were forced to retreat by oncoming darkness and during their descent, one member of the party was caught in a fatal avalanche. In 1974 a four-man team successfully completed a winter ascent via this route after spending four days on the ridge.

Retrace your route to descend from the summit of La Plata. Novice climbers sometimes try to bolt downhill. This haste is very stressful to knees and increases the risk of a tumble. It is best to come down in a deliberate, controlled manner to keep your body in good shape for the next climb.

Capitol Lake

TRAILHEAD:	24.4 miles from Mill & Main in Aspen
	21.1 miles from rodeo grounds in Snowmass Village
HIKING DISTANCE:	12.6 miles round trip to lake
	14.5 miles round trip to pass south of lake
	13.9 miles round trip to saddle between Capitol and Daly
ELEVATION GAIN:	2,580 feet to lake
	3,020 feet to pass
	3,460 feet to saddle between Capitol and Daly
HIGH POINT:	11,600 feet at lake
	12,040 feet at pass
	12,480 feet at saddle
HIGHLIGHTS:	Lovely, large alpine lake at foot of Capitol Peak
	A gradually ascending trail with abundant wildflowers
	Cheerful Capitol Creek alongside the route
	Two worthy sidetrips from the lakeshore

Comments: The journey to Capitol Lake has few rivals for scenic pleasures en route and satisfaction at the goal. It is a truly wonderful dayhike. And for those with extra energy and ambition, the sidetrips are highly recommended as they afford sights of less-accessible places in the wilderness. This is a long hike but not a grueling one as steep sections of trail alternate with level portions. The footing is mostly dirt, not rocks. A minor downside may be the 400 feet of elevation lost at the hike's very beginning. "Elevation gain" numbers above reflect this initial descent. The early lowland miles of the Capitol Lake hike can sometimes be muddy and manure-splotched. Horses use this trail, and cattle graze here.

Aspen to Trailhead: Proceed west from Aspen on route 82 noting the signs for Snowmass Village at the Brush Creek Road intersection. It is 8.5 miles from here to your turnoff at old Snowmass. Exit left from 82, drive for 1.8 miles, and turn right at the intersection of Snowmass Creek Road and Capitol Creek Road. Follow Capitol Creek Road, pass a left turn for St. Benedict Monastery, and head directly toward a rocky, snow-spotted expanse that stretches from Mt. Sopris near Carbondale to Capitol Peak. The road deteriorates to dirt at 6.5 miles from route 82. A mile beyond is

CAPITOL
LAKE

a picturesque old barn on the right. Farther along is a parking area for those who haul horse trailers. At about nine miles from 82 the road becomes very rough. This place is a mile from the parking area for the Capitol Lake hike. Newer cars should probably stop here. A four-wheel-drive vehicle, a truck, or an old city car can likely be taken as far as the trailhead, which is clearly designated by a sign and open space for parking.

Trail Route: Pause a moment at this hike's beginning to survey the beauty of the landscape. Below is a verdant dale glittering with creek, marsh, and ponds. Wending up the long valley, the creek leads to austere, gray Capitol Peak, a distinctive marker in the wilderness. The trail accompanies this creek after its 400-foot drop down a dusty slope fragrant with sagebrush and dotted with dry meadow flowers. Before reaching the marshy valley floor, the path crosses a water diversion ditch via logs and travels from sagebrush hillside to aspen woods. Such are the contrasts in the Rockies.

As the aspens thin out near a meadow, the trail

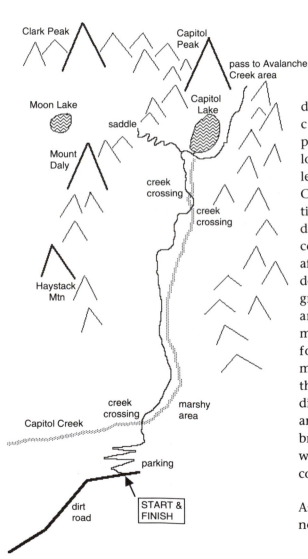

76

forks. Go right, traversing the flowery field where a colony of ground squirrels has tunneled subterranean homes. This damp bottomland has a confusion of both old and new trails. Logs placed across paths are signs of closure. At meadow's end small tree trunks form a primitive bridge to the trail's left. This facilitates the crossing of Capitol Creek, deep and swift in early summer. Beyond the creek enter spruce woods, begin a short uphill, and encounter, at the junction of an old trail and the new one, a Maroon Bells-Snowmass Wilderness sign. You are soon on a level dirt trail bordered by aspens. The route proceeds to a ridge high above a wide wet area where beavers have been at work and where the creek spreads out in channels. Across the valley are the red soil, red rocks, and snowy red pass of the Hell Roaring trail.

After about 45 minutes of hiking, a sidestream cuts the trail. Flamboyant and untidy, orange sneezeweed mixes among the aspens. Capitol Creek rushes alongside, splashing in whitewater falls and singing its lively song. A few minutes past the sidestream, the trail exits the woods, emerging into a vast meadow where the sight ahead is of Capitol Peak and, left of the summit, K2, its famous knob. A waterfall sparkles on the field's far side, mounds of disturbed earth suggest the labor of northern pocket gophers, and pale yellow northern paintbrush blooms everywhere.

The trail continues to parallel the creek, which descends in noisy rapids, and in about 30 minutes, crosses a vigorous tributary before emerging into another open area. The hillsides are covered in wildflowers and conifers.

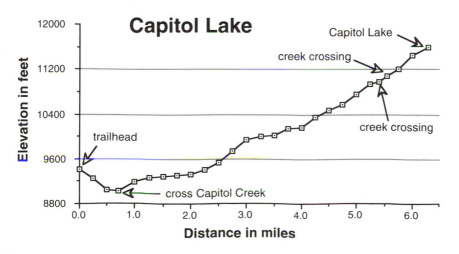

Aspens have been left behind, signaling a change in life zone. The grand view of Capitol Peak is repeated here, and pearly everlasting surrounds the trail.

In another 15 minutes the path dips down to the water. It is here that an alternate trail, approaching from across the creek, joins the Forest Service trail to Capitol Lake. Horses make the ford easily, but the creek is an obstacle for hikers. The alternate route, traversing the ridge above the valley, begins at the far side of the parking area and travels gently over open slopes and through pastures and aspen woods. This spot is slightly short of the hike's halfway point.

A beaver pond is just beyond the unmarked trail junction, and another huge meadow, purple with lupine, gives glorious sight of the mountain ahead. A short stretch of conifers precedes a massive avalanche area—a graveyard of fallen trees. The dirt trail continues to move from meadow to forest several times before it passes over a sidestream. Wildflowers may be waist-high in the sunny natural gardens. Some steady climbing on switchbacks brings you to an open spot on the right which reveals all of lush Capitol Creek valley and layers of low distant ridges.

Ten minutes after the viewspot you cross both the creek and a sidestream on separate spans of huge logs. A "Closed for Revegetation" sign stands in the old camping area. With the creek now to your left, climb to a knoll where the trail can be seen winding ahead. A rockslide is on its right, and Mount Daly, colored a soft rosy red, is left. Much maroon king's crown blooms here in July. Many other moisture-lovers, including the primitive horsetail plant, flourish all along this route.

Resident rocks make easy work of another passage over Capitol Creek en route to the hike's final meadow, a place of low flowers so rich in number and variety that it seems cousin to a Persian rug. The meadow ends at a conifer-clothed mound. Capitol Lake is secreted behind it. To the right of Capitol Peak rises a jagged mountaintop which extends to a smooth snowy ridge. The rocks' colors are gray, apricot, rose red. At right the creek bubbles along as you move forward. The trail divides, with both a high and low road, and reunites quickly. Melting snowfields may be present. Walk over rocks, jump water in a gully, traverse some flat ground, pass left of a boulder pile, and regard Capitol Lake. The vision is breath-taking.

The lake appears almost circular and, on a bright day, deep teal in color. In the shallows near shore, the sun imparts a turquoise hue. Across the water lies a pass, a low point in the lake's rocky embrace. To the pass's left is the handsome vertical face of Capitol Peak; to its right is a grassy slope. The rugged gray pinnacles and smooth ridge seen earlier rise farther to the right. Fat relaxed marmots exude a confidence that comes from knowing the territory better than the human invaders.

A narrow trail edges the lake's right shore and takes the traveler gradually upward over a rockfall, snowfields, and grass on the easy one-mile journey to the pass. From the trail hikers may spy climbers on the knife-edge approach to Capitol Peak. Mount Daly is fully in view. And from the pass the enormous valley cut by Avalanche Creek extends west to a wide expanse of distant snowy mountain peaks and to Avalanche Pass, a dayhike destination approached from the Crystal River valley. Here hide splendid, less-familiar trails of the wilderness.

A shorter but more vigorous sidetrip is the steep ascent east to the saddle between Capitol Peak and Mount Daly. It begins immediately left of the main trail's arrival at the lake. The track is visible from below and serves climbers who attempt treacherous Capitol Peak. The saddle offers an aerial view of secluded Moon Lake, snug against Mount Daly's side and isolated by a vast field of humongous boulders. To the northeast, beyond and below this bleak moonscape, is the green valley carved by West Snowmass Creek, born at Moon Lake.

Wildflower enthusiasts are certain to find satisfaction on this trip, as the diversity in terrain—dry slope, marsh, forest, tundra—offers a wealth of specimens in midsummer. At least a dozen tiny, but showy, alpine varieties hug the thin soil at the windswept pass. Waist-high delphinium, wild carrot, and chimingbells adorn lower, moist meadowlands. Rare wood nymph and bog pyrola bloom shyly in shadowy woods where they bow their faces toward the earth. Sego lily and narrowleaf paintbrush brighten dusty hillsides. This hike is a botanical and visual feast.

Pierre Lakes

TRAILHEAD:	14.2 miles from Mill & Main in Aspen
	5.5 miles from rodeo grounds in Snowmass Village
HIKING DISTANCE:	14.5 miles round trip
ELEVATION GAIN:	3,860 feet
HIGH POINT:	12,280 feet
HIGHLIGHTS:	Beautiful Bear Creek Falls
	Large lakes in gigantic rocky basin at foot of Capitol Peak
	Peace and solitude of a little-traveled area

Comments: This difficult hike demands physical fitness and mental alertness. A mere 600 feet of elevation is gained in its first 3.5 miles, making the journey seem deceptively easy. But the first real obstacle, a tricky crossing of Snowmass Creek, begins a series of challenges. Three major boulderfields and numerous steep sections of trail, including a near-vertical ascent of 600 feet, require endurance and agility; and the hike beyond the crossing necessitates excellent pathfinding skills as it is not maintained by the U.S. Forest Service. An early start is requisite as the hike can take 11 to 12 hours round trip. Deep in the Maroon Bells-Snowmass Wilderness, the lakes' locale is a formidable alpine environment that dwarfs man with its size, permanence, and austerity. It is an awesome place.

Aspen to Trailhead: Head west (downvalley) from Aspen on route 82. Turn left from 82 onto Brush Creek Road, the route to Snowmass Village, at 6.0 miles from Mill and Main in Aspen. Follow scenic Brush Creek Road and keep to the right when you reach the rodeo grounds at the lower end of Snowmass Village. Just beyond the golf course, pass under a wooden bridge and continue straight ahead through an intersection near a small business center. You reach Divide Road 0.5 miles beyond the wooden bridge. Stay to the right and drive 0.9 miles on Divide Road until reaching a dirt road at the Krabloonik kennels.

Follow the winding, rutted road down into the valley. If you have a city car, drive slowly and choose your way carefully to avoid prominent rocks and deep furrows. Several hundred yards past the bottom of the hill is the intersection with a dirt road from Old Snowmass (an alternate access route from Basalt, Carbondale, or Glenwood Springs). It is 1.5 miles from Krabloonik to the intersection. Continue straight ahead past a trailhead on your left for the East Snowmass Creek trail. Proceed another few hundred yards to a large dirt parking area.

Trail Route: A metal gate at the west side of the parking area is the point of departure. Hike the road to Snowmass Falls Ranch for about ten minutes until you spot a trail leading up an incline into the trees on your left. A wooden sign reading "Maroon Snowmass Trail No. 1975" marks the turnoff. Hazards may present themselves early on this adventure in the form of obstructive cattle, their fly-covered "pies", and, after a rain, boot-swallowing, red mud. The soft dirt pathway gains elevation gradually through light woods dotted with blue columbines. This terrain is conducive to a vigorous pace. If you wish to linger at the lakes, this stretch is the place to move along smartly. The blue-white turbulence

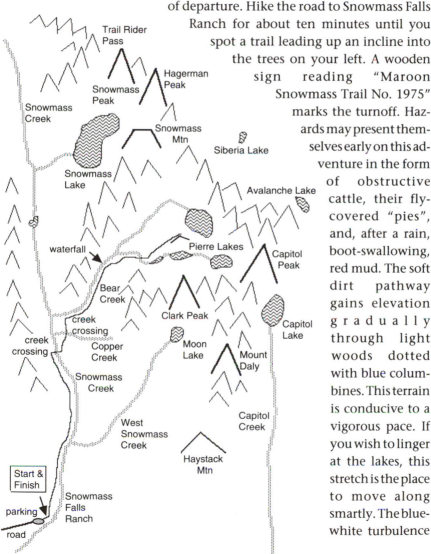

81

of Snowmass Creek is your noisy companion here and for the first 3.5 miles of the trek.

Twenty minutes after turning off the ranch road you approach a pond and a beaver dam. Just beyond the pond is the first of two log ranch gates. (Carefully close this and all gates across hiking trails.) Stinging nettles grow abundantly from here to the wilderness sign ahead. A shoulder of Snowmass Mountain rises in the distance. Soon the trail skirts a boggy area by climbing up and down a rough slope. Beyond the bog a small rockfield overlooks another beaver pond to the path's right. A sign reading "West Snowmass Trail" stands between the first gate and the second about 10 minutes farther along. (This trail takes hikers across the creek to Haystack Mountain or, on an unmaintained branch trail, to Moon Lake.) Shortly beyond the second ranch gate a wooden sign announces the boundary of the Maroon Bells-Snowmass Wilderness.

About 75 to 90 minutes into the trip, you pass alongside a small meadow on your left distinguished by a giant red boulder in its center. The big rock is a curious host to a variety of green, growing things. The standing trunk of a lightning-struck tree is its lifeless neighbor. Above the meadow rises the boulder's parent, a red sawtooth ridge, uplifted diagonally. At meadow's end a small wooden campsite sign to the trail's left marks the creek-crossing spot for the unidentified Pierre Lakes Trail. A small open place on your right sits between the trail and the creek. Be alert here as small signs sometimes

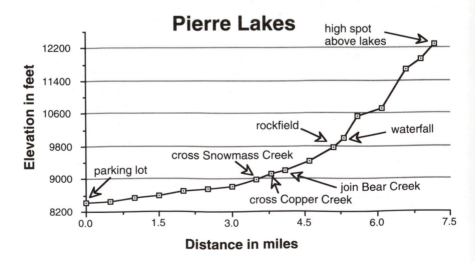

disappear. If you reach an area where the trail leaves the creek and gains elevation more rapidly, you have gone too far. The water-crossing is approximately 3.5 miles from the hike's start.

Snowmass Creek is swift and wide at this point. Fallen trees and branches may make a helpful span, but these can be wet and slippery. Use caution and offer assistance to companions. The creek, once bridged, parallels the trail at left. A pond, complete with a beaver lodge, is just beyond the crossing. The route is unmaintained and overgrown with bushes and evergreens, muddy in places and strewn with rocks and broken branches. The wetness of these woods supports horsetail, cow parsnip, and pearly everlasting. The path bisects a small meadow and then winds through spruces and aspens. Fifteen minutes after the turnoff for Pierre Lakes you hopscotch over Copper Creek, shallow and broad. Continue through a mixed forest with its undergrowth of tall plants. The trail is something of a roller coaster, dipping and rising.

As you approach Bear Creek the footpath angles to the right and follows the water upstream toward the falls. Pass through a meadow of bedstraw and yarrow with Bear Creek on your left. Soon the trail edges a picturesque, mini-canyon cut by the creek. A jagged, tilted, grayish ridge looms far above the canyon wall on your left. The ridge separates this valley from that of Snowmass Creek to the east. Moving slightly away from the creek, walk through a flowery meadow where you sight snow on the backside of the broad Snowmass mountain complex: Snowmass Mountain, Hagerman Peak, and Snowmass Peak. This location is about two hours into the hike. In the next clearing you view Bear Creek waterfall, a beautiful landmark that is easily seen from the Snowmass Lake trail.

The path continues to be indistinct, passing through closely-spaced trees and shrubs. About an hour after crossing Snowmass Creek and 5.1 miles into the hike, you begin to pick your way across a mammoth rockfield where the obstacles range in size from large gravel to boulders. Cairns mark the route, and a clump of trees divides the field into two parts. Bear Creek Falls is the view ahead. Exit the rockslide and search among bushes for an obscure turn directing hikers uphill to the right. The cataract is far left as you ascend sharply. At one rare flat lookout point you can detect a large mine entrance in the lower rock face left of the waterfall.

Next you encounter "the wall", a 600-foot vertical climb paralleling the falls, now out of sight. No trail seems possible here. The ascent requires hands and feet, tree roots and tree trunks, rock projections and steady nerves. The initial section is basic non-technical rock climbing requiring some giant steps. Ledges, deep cracks, and occasional trees offer aid. The wooded upper section is a series of verticals alternating with level places. Stay on the trail. Straying off course can place you a step away from a sudden descent or a ledge from which there is no escape except by retracing your path.

At the crest of the wall you meet Bear Creek before its plunge creates the lovely cascade seen from below. Make careful note of the trail's characteristics near the wall's top edge as you must return by exactly the same route. There are no safe alternatives. Tie a strip of cloth to a tree or stack rocks to mark the spot where you must descend later in the day.

Above the falls is a flat woodland trail through conifers. The place is home to mushrooms and shade-loving flowers: bog pyrola, pipsissewa, wood nymph. But the way is faint, and there are many distracting side trails leading to campsites. The comfortable soft dirt path soon gives way to a trek across another rockfield. This expanse is smaller than the one below, and its rocks are larger, more stable, and attired in colorful lichen. From this vantage point you have a stunning view of the snow-covered backside of Snowmass.

The trail above the falls is occasionally ill-defined. If you seem to be bushwhacking, explore until you find the trodden pathway. There is a trail, however faded, all the way to the lake area.

Beyond the rocks is a gentle uphill walk through evergreens interrupted by open spots. Much sickletop lousewort blooms here. A pretty creek and meadow area follows where among the tall grasses are spikes of purple monkshood and, in August, a variety of gentians. A rockslide is ahead. Move left across the slide and face a long steep climb up a hill bordered by conifers and talus slopes and paved with huge white boulders and fallen tree trunks. The land drops off to the left. Peachy-gray, needle-sharp ridges rear above you. When partway up the hill, bear to the right at the cairn. Continue directly upward through some grass and over more fallen trees. There are no switchbacks here to mitigate the elevation gain of nearly a thousand feet. Aim for the hill's crown where the conifers thin out, a signal that treeline is nearby.

At the crown, bear right diagonally across a grassy space. Locate cairns for direction as you proceed up a rise overlooking another meadow, the best of the hike. A snowmelt stream sparkles through brightly-colored wildflowers: rosy paintbrush, red elephant heads, western yellow paintbrush, American bistort, penstemon, alpine anemone, brookcress, and alpine speedwell. The same needle-sharp ridge stands at right and connects, behind a green-clad meadow hump, to rounded Clark Peak. Walk straight toward Clark which is right of commanding Capitol Peak, whose knife-edge ridge links its summit to its knob, K2. The stream trickles under the trail as you continue to climb again. Soon the trail disappears, and it is time to depart the flowers to enter a world of harshness and austerity.

Leave the stream where it forms shallow ponds in a open space below the trail at right and bear to the left into a vast basin of gargantuan boulders. Capitol Peak is now directly ahead and the Snowmass complex is the giant to its left. Gray is the pre-eminent color in this place where, over the centuries, high peaks have dropped parts of themselves to build a moonscape. Scramble across the rocks toward the high point ahead which supports a few stubborn, twisted trees growing low and small. Remain left of Capitol's summit. You must climb over several knolls of boulders before reaching the place from which the largest of the Pierre Lakes is visible. Two smaller lakes can be located to your right as you step, hop, and clamber across the basin. The fourth lake is sequestered in a bowl beneath K2 at some distance from your location.

On achieving the high knoll with its valiant trees sprouting miraculously from stones, you are positioned for a splendid 360-degree panorama. Above and around you are Clark and two fourteeners, Capitol and Snowmass. Before you stretches the largest of the four lakes. A tarn nestles below the knoll. Through a notch in the surrounding mountains, the dark red summit of one of the Maroon Bells rises in contrast to the gray of nearby peaks. Behind some distant red ridges to the rear of the Bells is a glimpse of Cathedral Peak. Nature here is neither gentle nor kind. This is a severe and imposing place—a place to remind us of human frailty and insignificance.

Snowmass Lake and Trail Rider Pass

TRAILHEAD:	14.2 miles from Mill & Main in Aspen
	5.5 miles from rodeo grounds in Snowmass Village
HIKING DISTANCE:	17.0 miles round trip to Snowmass Lake
	20.6 miles round trip to Trail Rider Pass
ELEVATION GAIN:	2,580 feet to Snowmass Lake
	4,000 feet to Trail Rider Pass
HIGH POINT:	10,980 feet at Snowmass Lake
	12,420 feet at Trail Rider Pass
HIGHLIGHTS:	Delightful stream parallel to trail
	Snowmass Lake—an unforgettable, pristine jewel
	Magnificent, massive mountain peaks around lake
	Beautiful natural spillway
	Rainbow and cutthroat trout

Comments: This is a full-day hike. If you wish to linger at the lake or reach the pass, you should be at the trailhead shortly after sunrise. The trail is rocky in places and traverses some wet areas. It is not terrain for sneakers or tennis shoes; wear boots and carry spare socks. A major creek crossing late in the hike makes extra clothing another wise addition to your pack. Because of the distance and elevation gain, visitors should not attempt to complete this hike during their first three days in the high country.

Aspen to Trailhead: Head west (downvalley) from Aspen on route 82. Turn left from 82 onto Brush Creek Road, the route to Snowmass Village, at 6.0 miles from Mill and Main in Aspen. Follow scenic Brush Creek Road and keep to the right when you reach the rodeo grounds at the lower end of Snowmass Village. Just beyond the golf course, pass under a wooden bridge and continue straight ahead through an intersection near a small business center. You reach Divide Road 0.5 miles from the wooden bridge. Stay to the right and drive 0.9 miles on Divide Road until reaching a dirt road at the Krabloonik kennels.

Follow the winding, rutted road down into the valley. If you have a city car, drive slowly and choose your way carefully to avoid prominent rocks and deep furrows. Several hundred yards past the bottom of the hill is the intersection with a dirt road from Old Snowmass (an alternate access route from Basalt, Carbondale, or Glenwood Springs). It is 1.5 miles from Krabloonik to the intersection. Continue straight ahead past a trailhead on your left for the East Snowmass Creek trail. Proceed another few hundred yards to a large dirt parking area.

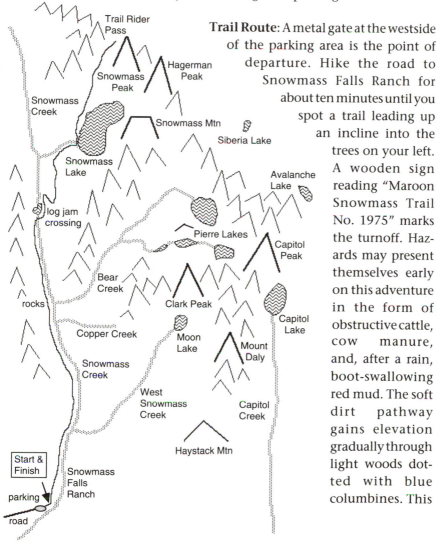

Trail Route: A metal gate at the westside of the parking area is the point of departure. Hike the road to Snowmass Falls Ranch for about ten minutes until you spot a trail leading up an incline into the trees on your left. A wooden sign reading "Maroon Snowmass Trail No. 1975" marks the turnoff. Hazards may present themselves early on this adventure in the form of obstructive cattle, cow manure, and, after a rain, boot-swallowing red mud. The soft dirt pathway gains elevation gradually through light woods dotted with blue columbines. This

87

SNOWMASS
LAKE
AND
TRAIL
RIDER
PASS

terrain is conducive to a vigorous pace. If you wish to tarry at the lake or attain Trail Rider Pass, this is a good time to move along smartly. The blue-white turbulence of Snowmass Creek is your noisy companion here and for the first 3.5 miles of the trek.

Twenty minutes after turning off the ranch road you approach a pond and a beaver dam. Just beyond the pond is the first of two log ranch gates. (Carefully close this and all gates across hiking trails.) Stinging nettles grow abundantly from here to the wilderness sign ahead. A shoulder of Snowmass Mountain rises in the distance. Soon the trail skirts a boggy area by climbing up and down a rough slope. Beyond the bog a small rockfield overlooks another beaver pond to the path's right. A sign reading "West Snowmass Trail" stands between the first gate and the second about 10 minutes farther along. (This trail takes hikers across the creek to Haystack Mountain or, on an unmaintained branch trail, to Moon Lake.) Shortly beyond the second ranch gate a wooden sign announces the boundary of the Maroon Bells-Snowmass Wilderness.

The trail continues along the stream for the first 3.5 miles of the hike. The trail then moves away from the stream and gains elevation more noticeably. Lying about in the airy aspen woods are huge granite boulders spotted with crustose orange lichens. Their massive bulk is in dramatic contrast to the delicate grasses and wild geraniums that grow here. You begin to climb more steeply. After another mile a group of large rocks borders the trail.

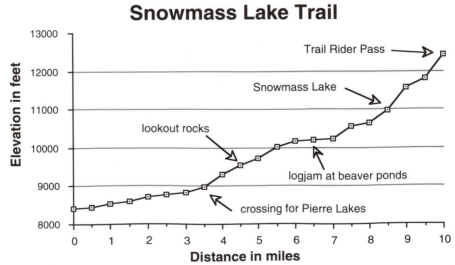

Snowmass Lake Trail

SNOWMASS
LAKE
AND
TRAIL
RIDER
PASS

This is a good spot for a breather and a chance to look out across the countryside. Across the valley Bear Creek cascades over a rocky precipice and snowcapped peaks loom in the background. The challenging trail to Pierre Lakes climbs the wall to the right of this cataract.

Beyond "look-out rocks" the trail continues to mount over rougher terrain, and about 30 minutes after the waterfall view, it rejoins Snowmass Creek. After moving through rockfields ornamented by purple fringe and raspberry bushes, you come upon other beaver dams in poor repair. The series of large, shallow ponds remaining are about a mile and a half past the lookout point. Most of the aspens have been harvested, and the beavers may have moved on to a more favorable site. The trail levels out and skirts the left side of the pools, passing briefly through some cool woods of conifers and berry bushes. The marshy environment near these lagoons encourages the growth of horsetail, kings crown, and chimingbells. Two-thirds of the way around the ponds (about 0.5 miles), the trail traverses a large logjam. This water-crossing, the only one on the trip, is about 6.5 miles from the trailhead. In early summer or after a rainfall, the logs can be wet and slippery. The crossing is not difficult, but every summer a few careless hikers find themselves wet and cold far from the trailhead.

The first reward on the creek's opposite side is a spectacular July flowering of blue sky pilots. The trail meanders along the right side of the ponds until it reaches the far end. Here the hiker ascends an open ridge by a series of switchbacks. Vivid yellow buckwheat blankets the nearby meadow. The route crosses sidestreams, enters a conifer forest, and marches upward more gradually. In the trees the trail bends gently to the right around another ridge. About two miles from the logjam, the hiker encounters a wooden sign with an arrow pointing straight ahead for Snowmass Lake and another pointing left for the trail to Buckskin Pass and Maroon Lake. Proceed toward Snowmass Lake. Soon Snowmass Creek is alongside to the trail's left, and it is splendid—a tumult of sparkling whitewater plunging down a rocky bed, a clue to the size of the lake beyond. Then—waterfalls. Some are lacy snowmelt rivulets. Two are bountiful cascades. The second rushes over a perfect, terraced rock spillway. This spot is a worthy destination, but the lake lies within sight, and it is wonderful: immense, glistening, dark, deep, pristine—and held like a jewel in a giant's cupped hand.

Snowmass
Lake
AND
Trail
Rider
Pass

Upon reaching the lake, you can cross some logs at the outlet to proceed along the shoreline to your left. A short way from the crossing you have perspective on the tremendous size of the lake and the surrounding mountains. Everything here, except the wildflowers, is on an enormous scale. Snowmass Mountain to the right is indeed the goliath, towering white and majestic over its liquid treasure. Connected to its left is Hagerman Peak, and rising to Hagerman's left is Snowmass Peak. On the rugged ridge to the left, or southeast, of Snowmass Peak is the depression that is Trail Rider Pass. The high expanse to the left of Trail Rider extends back toward Maroon Bells. Snowmelt streams from the mountains are audible across the lake's breadth. The summit of mammoth Snowmass Mountain soars to 14,092 feet. It is one of the more difficult climbs of the 54 fourteeners in Colorado.

The 8.5 mile trek to the lake usually takes three to four hours for those who hike along steadily.

Trail Rider Pass: If the skies are clear, the day is early, and members of your party are eager for another challenge, Trail Rider Pass is nearby. The view of Snowmass Lake from the pass is a visual delight. The climb is steep and demanding and should not be undertaken unless hikers are prepared for vigorous physical exertion. The trail to the lake climbs 2,500 feet in 8.5 miles; the trek from the lake to the pass rises another 1,400 feet in just 1.8 miles. The pass is exposed and should not be attempted if storm clouds are threatening.

To reach the pass, start from the campsite area that is reached by crossing the outlet as you enter the lake region. Proceed away from the lake while scouting for a faint track that enters the trees above. Within a few minutes you encounter a well-trodden trail perpendicular to your direction of movement. Join this trail and move uphill to the right. Very shortly you are on a bluff high above the water. The trail continues its ascent, traverses a large rockfield, and reaches alpine tundra. The trees are small and huddle in semi-sheltered areas. For the next mile the trail mounts across exposed tundra and then switchbacks sharply on the final approach to the ridge.

From Trail Rider Pass you look south into a deep valley carved by glaciers and the North Fork of the Crystal River. The valley beyond and perpendicular to the river is verdant Hasley Basin. The distant summits are Galena

SNOWMASS
LAKE
AND
TRAIL
RIDER
PASS

Mountain at left, Treasury Mountain, and Treasure Mountain at right. Rising in the foreground just in front of these peaks are Crystal Peak, Bear Mountain, and Little Bear Mountain. Looking back from the pass, you can spy Snowmass Lake nestled far below in the basin encircled by its mammoth protectors. If the day is sunny, the water will gleam like a gemstone. Burn these vistas deep into your memory. The vastness of the view, the fragrance of the mountain air, and the satisfaction of reaching this remote wilderness ridge can never be captured by clicking a camera shutter.

East Maroon-Conundrum Half-Circle

TRAILHEAD:	7.8 miles from Mill & Main in Aspen
	13.9 miles from rodeo grounds in Snowmass Village
HIKING DISTANCE:	19.8 miles for half-circle trip
ELEVATION GAIN:	4,240 feet
HIGH POINT:	12,900 feet at Triangle Pass
HIGHLIGHTS:	Two parallel scenic valleys plus two alpine passes
	Splendid vista from Triangle Pass
	Conundrum Hot Springs as midday respite
	Upper basins resplendent with wildflowers

Comments: This full-day adventure requires two cars or a single car plus hitchhiking. The preferred method is to deposit one vehicle at the Conundrum trailhead the night before the planned hike. To do this proceed west for 1.3 miles on route 82 from Mill and Main in Aspen. Turn left onto Maroon Creek Road at the traffic light and chapel and take an immediate left onto Castle Creek Road. Drive 4.8 miles and look for a right-hand turn onto a descending dirt road. Follow this road for 1.1 miles past some houses until it ends in the parking area for the Conundrum trailhead. Leave the car here to provide transportation after your trek the next day. You might place a cooler of liquids inside to relieve any dehydration incurred during this lengthy trip.

The hike starts at the parking lot and bridge for the East Maroon Creek trail. Begin at an early hour. The access road to the trailhead is closed to private vehicular traffic at 8:30 a.m. And as the journey is long, it is wise to cover the early miles while the air is cool and invigorating. It is prudent also to be over the second pass before afternoon storms menace. A bonus of the early start is the added time for a relaxing soak in the hot springs. Bring sport sandals or old sneakers for wading across East Maroon Creek. There are two difficult fords, and they are best attempted late in the summer season when the water level is lowest. This hike's mileage suggests a full daypack with safety items, rain gear, and extra food and water.

EAST
MAROON-
CONUN-
DRUM
HALF-
CIRCLE

Aspen to Trailhead: After leaving a car at the Conundrum trailhead (directions above), drive a second vehicle to the intersection of route 82 and Maroon Creek Road. Turn left from route 82 and go straight ahead for 3.2 miles to the stop sign at the T-Lazy-7 ranch. Continue past the ranch on Maroon Creek Road for another 3.1 miles where, just beyond the Silver Queen campground, is the turn-off at left for the East Maroon Creek trail. Drive 0.2 miles down this dirt road to a parking area where there may be trailers unloading horses. To reach the trailhead cross the wooden bridge at the end of the parking lot.

Trail Route: The broad track up the East Maroon Creek Valley is well-defined and climbs very gently for the first five miles. The plentiful fly-flecked droppings along the route testify to its popularity with the equestrian crowd. Buzzing horseflies are unpleasant trail companions. But the nippy air of post-dawn hours keeps these voracious biters locked in a stupor while encouraging hikers to march along.

The hike's initial eight miles parallel East Maroon Creek. After the first mile or so, a distinct trail descends to the right. It drops to the creek, crosses a sturdy wooden bridge, and meanders along West Maroon Creek to the Maroon Bells campground area. Continue straight ahead at this

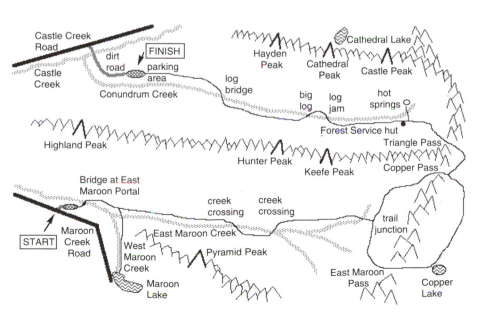

EAST
MAROON-
CONUN-
DRUM
HALF-
CIRCLE

intersection. As the trail climbs, pleasant creek noises are far below on your right. Four miles into your ascent the backside of Pyramid Peak dominates the view directly across the valley. Nearby are the remains of two long-abandoned cabins.

Just past the 5.5-mile point lies a zone where avalanches (snow slides) have flattened much of an aspen grove. And a slight distance ahead is the first creek crossing. The water moves rapidly, numbs with its chill, and, in spots, is more than knee-deep. Here is a place to remove boots and socks and to don old sneakers before wading. In early summer this ford can be danger-ous. Once over the creek, continue up the valley with the water to your left. Expect some wetness and mud underfoot. Approximately one mile beyond the first crossing, the trail again fords the creek. This ford is also difficult, and the sneaker trick is recommended once more.

On the opposite bank, the trail mounts through a rocky region where the path steepens noticeably. The route proceeds uphill through forest and, eventually, at 8.3 miles from the trailhead, reaches an intersection. The trail to the right guides hikers to East Maroon Pass, slightly more than a mile ahead, and then descends to Copper Lake. Continue to the right about 50 feet past this intersection where a small waterfall invites a pause for a rest and an energizing snack.

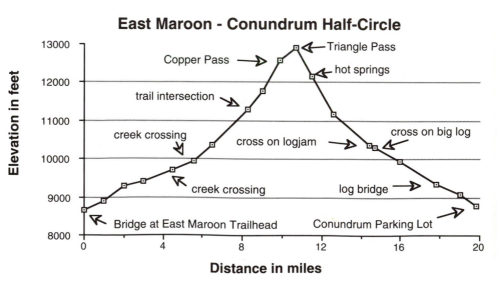

East Maroon - Conundrum Half-Circle

East
Maroon-
Conun-
drum
Half-
Circle

To reach Copper Pass, Triangle Pass, and Conundrum Hot Springs, back-track to the intersection and follow the trail heading left. You soon enter a capacious upper valley, refuge for much wildlife. Deer are often sighted here. The path traverses the valley, moving toward Copper Pass. Some-times the route is indistinct. Scout for cairns (rock piles) that mark the way. In addition, scan the ridge ahead for a saddle, a low place that demarcates the pass. In attaining the alpine region of this high basin, you leave all trees behind. Copper Pass is 1.6 miles beyond the trail intersection and 9.9 miles from the trailhead.

The trail advances over the pass and drops briefly, intersecting with another trail climbing along the ridge. This path leading down and to the right is a rock-strewn route to Copper Lake. Instead, keep left, going across the basin ahead, and in a few minutes, climbing a ridge to Triangle Pass. Triangle Pass is only 0.8 miles beyond Copper Pass and is 320 feet higher at 12,900 feet. If you set off in the very early morning and travel at a steady pace, you should arrive at Triangle Pass by noon. The Colorado mountains attract frequent summer afternoon thunderstorms so it is best to reach the high point of any hike before ominous clouds gather. Crossing a high ridge in a lightning storm is a good way to turn yourself into charcoal.

From Triangle Pass stretches a wonderful view of the Conundrum valley, enlivened by a creek and embellished with hot springs. Above the valley craggy Castle and Cathedral peaks exhibit their less-familiar facades. Triangle is the second-highest named pass in the Elk Mountains. Only Electric Pass is loftier.

Descending the ridge, you enter Conundrum valley. The upper section is a grand basin well above treelimit where, in July and early August, wildflowers bloom in a breath-taking display. The trail drops rapidly toward Conundrum Hot Springs. A U.S. Forest Service hut stands 1.9 miles below the pass. Just before the hut, a trail leading right crosses a small stream en route to the hot springs. The two soaking areas are both visible from the main trail. You are likely to encounter other hikers at the springs and might approach cautiously if you are uncomfortable with nudity.

The hot springs are welcome refreshment for weary legs and sore feet. At a distance of 12.5 miles from the starting trailhead, the springs are nicely located to provide a relaxing place for food, conversation, and

EAST
MAROON-
CONUN-
DRUM
HALF-
CIRCLE

rejuvenation. Most of the difficult hiking is behind you, and it is time to replenish energy stores. You are about 3.5 hours from the Conundrum parking lot and should time your departure with this in mind.

The trail descending from the hot springs wends through a picturesque valley lavish with flora and fauna. At 1.8 miles from the Forest Service hut, you must clamber over Conundrum Creek on a jumble of sticks and logs. Though not difficult, the task is awkward, and a careless move begets wet feet. Beyond this tangle, the trail passes a large pond and traverses the creek again, this time on a very large and very steady log. The distance between these two crossings is about 0.4 miles. The path drifts gradually downhill. A third creek crossing waits 3.1 miles below the second. But there is no challenge here as two logs placed side-by-side constitute a tidy "bridge".

Walk an old four-wheel-drive road for another two miles to the parking lot. You have covered 19.8 miles and climbed up and down a 4,200-foot elevation change. Fatigue is usual after such a physical day at high elevation. But mountain memories and the satisfaction of real accomplishment can be compensation.

Fravert Basin Loop

TRAILHEAD:	10.9 miles from Mill & Main in Aspen
	17.0 miles from rodeo grounds in Snowmass Village
HIKING DISTANCE:	23.4 miles for full loop trip
ELEVATION GAIN:	7,360 feet
HIGH POINT:	12,500 feet at West Maroon Pass
HIGHLIGHTS:	Expansive views from four mountain passes
	The waterfall, flowers, and peace of Fravert Basin
	Snowmass Lake and its surrounding peaks
	Major physical challenge

Comments: This trail is long and arduous, carrying hikers through a remote region of the wilderness. It should not be attempted by anyone who is not in superb physical condition. Hikers should leave Maroon Lake at dawn and should be prepared to return by flashlight if necessary. A brisk pace is essential. The trek is best undertaken in late July or early August when days are still long and mountain passes are clear of heavy snow. Rain gear and extra pairs of dry socks are required baggage. Each hiker should have a minimum of six pints of fluid for drinking. Several trail guides classify this four-pass loop as a three- to five-day backpacking trip.

Aspen to Trailhead: Drive west 1.3 miles from Mill and Main in Aspen to the traffic light and chapel at the intersection of Route 82 and Maroon Creek Road. Turn left from 82 and keep right as the road makes an immediate fork. Drive 9.6 miles up Maroon Creek Road to the parking area nestled below Pyramid Peak and the Maroon Bells.

Trail Route: This adventure begins with an ascent of the heavily-traveled path from Maroon Lake to Crater Lake. Just before Crater Lake the trail bisects at the Forest Service register. Sign the register and indicate your intended route and return time. Walk straight ahead toward the lake at this junction. The trail mounting to the right heads for Buckskin Pass. You will hike down the Buckskin Pass trail on your return later in the day.

Tread along the right shore of Crater Lake and bear slightly right into woods as you hike up the valley toward West Maroon Pass. The trail traverses several boggy areas and then passes across, above, and below several enormous rock slides. Pyramid Peak and the Maroon Bells tower over everything, giants in this wild landscape. About 2.5 miles from the trailhead you must cross West Maroon Creek. It is broad and shallow, and hikers usually hop over the flow on rocks or logs. After another three-quarters of a mile, it is time to cross again. Here, where the creek is narrower and deeper, reaching the other bank may be more of a challenge. Try moving upstream a short distance to scout for a better crossing place. Beyond this obstacle the dirt trail bends to the right side of the valley and climbs a sloping meadow festooned with purple lupine and red elephant heads. This area is renowned for its show of wildflowers.

As you advance toward the head of the valley, look for a small saddle on the right of the ridge ahead. This is West Maroon pass, a rugged place of pinnacles and of layered red rocks tilted rakishly. The trail steers toward the pass, ascending a wide rolling meadow dampened by a little stream. Snakelike, the trail approaches the ridgetop, making a series of switchbacks

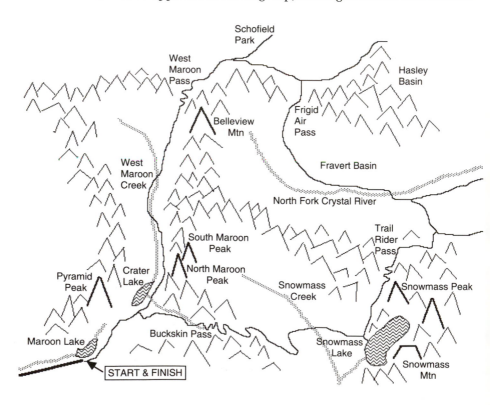

98

to reduce the steepness. From West Maroon Pass the territory through which you have just journeyed exhibits ragged spires and angled surfaces. But in the other direction, across Schofield Park toward Gothic and Crested Butte, the land is softened, rounded. Ridges flow into one another. There is a spaciousness and gentleness to the aspect.

At this juncture it is important to make a careful assessment. Check your watch and calculate the time taken to hike the 5.5 miles from the trailhead to the pass. If you have exceeded three hours, you are not moving rapidly enough to complete the loop before nightfall. You should also scrutinize the sky. You must cross three high mountain passes later in the day, and if thunderheads are moving your way, it is appropriate to alter your plans. West Maroon Pass is considered by many to be a desirable goal in itself.

If your pace is adequate and the sky conditions acceptable, drop down on the other side of the ridge. Once you depart West Maroon Pass, you are committed to the full loop. This decision should not be taken lightly.

The trail descends toward Schofield Park. At 1.1 miles below the pass there is a poorly-marked trail junction. If you miss it, you continue your travel down into the valley, taking the route to Crested Butte. Instead, go right at the intersection and move along the side of the valley parallel to the ridge above. The hillside dirt path is soft and fairly level, a place to make

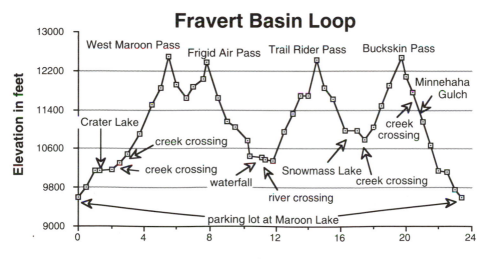

Fravert Basin Loop

good time. A great profusion of wildflowers extends in all directions. One mile from the trail junction, just past a small pond to your right, there is a second intersection, also inconspicuous. If you continue straight ahead, you journey to Hasley Basin. The proper loop route is to the right and up the ridge. At the top is Frigid Air Pass. The trail climbs sharply up the slope, testing the traction on your boots.

From the pass you gaze on the backside of the Maroon Bells, an uncommon and striking perspective. Frigid Air Pass also delivers an aerial view of the broad valley ahead, beautiful Fravert Basin. This basin hides in the heart of the Maroon Bells-Snowmass Wilderness and, because of its remoteness, is visited by few hikers. The North Fork of the Crystal River is born at the head of the valley on your right. The river is visible far below where it flows west (to your left) toward Crystal.

As you drop into Fravert Basin from Frigid Air Pass, the trail initially descends abruptly via switchbacks; it then falls more gradually as it aims for a grove of conifers at treeline. Soon you are among trees and guided toward the river. The sound of rushing water announces the North Fork. The trail, now on the riverbank, conducts you downstream. After about 1.5 miles you encounter a steep gorge, a place of rapids and an exquisite waterfall that cascades over rocks in a long plunge to the lower section of valley. The trail remains left of the waterfall and switchbacks through the woods as it descends.

Below the waterfall the vigorous river loses its energy. Moving slowly, it forms a series of small ponds. The trail gives a wide berth to the boggy pond area and continues down the valley. About a half-mile below the falls, the trail enters a large clearing where it intersects another path. At one time this clearing was the site of Love's Cabin. Very little remains of the cabin, and even the trail junction is indeterminate. The faint path approaching from the left is a route to Hasley Basin. Continuing straight ahead steers you downriver toward Crystal. The loop route goes to the right, aiming straight for the river. This obstacle is broad but fairly shallow (between ankle- and knee-deep) and is crossed by wading or by judicious rock-hopping.

Beyond the ford of the North Fork, the trail again directs you downstream along the river. A half-mile from the crossing is yet another junction. This turn-off is easy to miss. Though the main trail continues straight ahead, you should exit to the right and climb the hillside switchbacks. As you ascend into aspens, you gain an unobstructed view of the broad valley below. You are now starting the long and tiring climb to Trail Rider Pass. It is important to maintain a steady pace even if you are short of breath and your legs are screaming for a rest. You should reach Trail Rider at midday to complete the trek back to Maroon Lake before nightfall.

About 1.25 miles above the valley junction, just as you are reaching treeline, the trail divides again. The pathway at left leads to Geneva Lake. You should move uphill to the right. The trail mounts steadily, bears right over a rise, and then flattens out across a large upper basin. You pass several ponds as you traverse the basin. Ahead and to the left is a saddle atop a ridge. This is Trail Rider Pass, your next destination. You have expended considerable energy in reaching this place high above the North Fork of the Crystal River. But Trail Rider is still 600 feet higher. The trail steepens noticeably just beneath the pass, and a set of switchbacks carries you to the ridge.

The sights from Trail Rider Pass are something to savor. Behind you are the Fravert Basin and the mountains surrounding Crystal. Ahead and far below is shining Snowmass Lake, snug beneath the snowfields of Snowmass Peak, Hagerman, and Snowmass Mountain. If the weather is favorable, this is a good perch for a lunch break. Trail Rider is 14.5 miles from the hike's beginning. It is easy to justify a rest.

From Trail Rider the path drops sharply toward the lake. Walk across the tundra and into a rocky region. Follow a ridge above the lake and enjoy excellent views. About 1.6 miles below the pass, the trail moves away from this ridge and guides you through boulders and conifers. To the left a faint path wanders off into woods. This trail permits a side trip to Snowmass Lake. The detour is just over a tenth of a mile and is worth the time and energy. If you have never been to Snowmass Lake, a visit is mandatory. If you have been there before, a return trip is still a fine idea. Every interlude at Snowmass Lake is good for the soul.

From Snowmass Lake, there are two good routes back to civilization. The main loop trail crosses Buckskin Pass and descends via Crater Lake to Maroon Lake and the hike's beginning. If thunderheads and lightning threaten or if your party is unable to climb over another high pass, the popular trail down Snowmass Creek is an alternative. This route is entirely below treeline and descends gradually for 8.5 miles. It concludes at a large parking area where there is a chance for a ride into Snowmass Village. Buses run hourly from the village to Aspen.

To stay on the loop, retrace your steps from the lake to the main trail. Continue downhill, bearing to the right. Pass through a heavily-forested area and then enter a large open valley. The trail is fairly level here. You are hiking toward Snowmass Creek and can hear the dashing water as you approach. At one time a wooden bridge spanned the creek. No longer. The trail should lead you to a small gorge where a log connects the creek's banks. Beyond the crossing, continue along a hillside while staying parallel to the stream. After a half-mile, the trail turns into the woods and starts a long climb to Buckskin Pass. The trail is well-marked and easy to follow.

By now it is probably late afternoon, you are weary, and Buckskin Pass seems loftier than any fourteener. But the trail marches forward. Above treeline it steers you through alpine meadows and into rocky, open tundra. A final long switchback guides you to the pass. If you have made it this far without berating yourself or your companions for the idiocy of attempting such a dayhike, you are truly a special person. Buckskin Pass is the last major hurdle on your journey. It is all downhill from here. When you reach the pass, look behind you for a magnificent view of Snowmass Lake tucked below Snowmass Mountain. Directly ahead are the multiple snags of Pyramid Peak. The pass itself is attached to the shoulder of North Maroon, imposing in its immediacy just to your right.

The trail descending from Buckskin Pass shepherds you through a series of switchbacks into a large basin containing wildlife, flowers, and a frisky mountain stream. Halfway down is another crossroads. The left path conveys hikers over Willow Pass to Willow Lake. Keeping to the right, head downhill toward an opening. The trail joins the stream, and together they exit the basin, dropping into a conifer forest. The trail twists and turns and then crosses a creek on its way toward Crater Lake. There is a roar to your right as water plummets noisily through Minnehaha Gulch. Continue on the main route, ignoring the many spurs that lead to campsites.

At 1.3 miles from the trail intersection, Crater Lake can be spotted below through trees and off to the right. In another mile you reach Crater and connect with the trail that you traveled just after sunrise. Turn left on the main trail and hike the final 1.6 miles to Maroon Lake and the parking lot. This excursion, like other lengthy treks, is best concluded by dipping into a cache of cold drinks in your car.

FRAVERT
BASIN
LOOP

Beasts & Birds

"What is man without the beasts? If all the beasts were gone, men would die from great loneliness of spirit, for whatever happens to the beasts also happens to man. All things are connected. Whatever befalls the earth befalls the children of the earth."

—Seattle, chief of the Suqwamish and Duwamish

Beasts & Birds

O NE OF THE GREAT PLEASURES OF WILDERNESS HIKING IS THE OBSERVATION OF wilderness residents. Colorado's Elk Mountains are home to many wild things, but most native creatures are shy and wary; some prefer precipitous cliffs or remote ridges; others are abroad only at night; and a few are true earth-dwellers, rarely emerging from underground tunnels and burrows. Yet there exist bold and nonchalant individuals who startle and delight. And dayhikers can substantially increase their wildlife sightings by learning where to look, by maintaining a quiet presence on the trail, and by setting forth in the very early morning.

So while many alpine mammals and birds are scarce and secretive, others are abundant and accessible. The wild animals introduced in this hiking guide are those who readily reveal themselves, those who leave physical evidence of their existence, and those who best represent the special environment of the mountains. A more extensive study of alpine wildlife requires one of the comprehensive field guides available in Aspen bookstores.

Small Mammals

Many of the animals met along the trail are of the endearing, small furry variety. And while some are quick to sound shrill warnings or to scurry under rockpiles, others may choose to study intruding humans or to solicit scraps from a backpack lunch.

Generously striped, highly vocal, and abundant in numbers, tiny adaptable **chipmunks** live in forests, on mountainsides, and in sagebrush deserts. They nest in burrows and in trees. The 19 western species (*Eutamias*) look very much alike. From nose to tip of tail they measure 6.5 to 9.0 inches in length. Their ranges overlap, and their subtle color variations allow them to meld with their specific terrains. Chipmunks have large internal cheek pouches for carrying seeds and berries and are distinguished by multiple stripes running from rump to nose.

Resembling an oversize chipmunk, the **golden-mantled ground squirrel** (*Spermophilus lateralis*) gets its common name from the reddish-gold color of its head and shoulders. Strictly a high-altitude, burrowing squirrel, it is found from 7,000 feet of elevation to far above treeline. It has fewer stripes than the chipmunk, and those stripes end at the shoulder. But like the smaller chipmunk, the golden-mantled ground squirrel has cheek pouches and stores food for wakeful moments during winter hibernation. Overall length of the animal is 9.0 to 12.0 inches. Numerous, active, and outgoing, this ground squirrel may approach humans for tidbits of food.

A busy, conspicuous resident of rockslides, the mottled, grayish-brown **pika** (*Ochotona princeps*) has no time for people. The pika is shaped much like a guinea pig and colored much like its environment. Although a member of the rabbit family, the pika has short round ears and no visible tail. (Diminished extremities are less likely to freeze in alpine winters.) And unlike its larger rabbit and hare cousins, the pika is active by day, lives in large sociable colonies, and communicates noisily with piping squeaks that can be heard at a distance. The pika has fur on the soles of its feet, making a nonskid activity of

pika

its sprints over stones. Smaller than the pygmy rabbit, this mountain relative has a body length of 6.5 to 8.5 inches.

The pika lives only in rockfields near meadows from below treelimit to elevations of 13,500 feet. It spends summer months industriously harvesting grasses, sedges, and wildflowers which are dried in low haystacks. Later stored in dens beneath the rocks, the dried vegetation sustains the energetic pika who does not hibernate. Couples cooperate to raise one or two litters during the summer but retreat to separate burrows in winter. This flashing fur ball has many nicknames, including cony, whistling hare, piping hare, and little chief hare. Locating a pika by his shrill voice can be difficult. Rockfields may distort the cry. And the animal's practice of jerking its body upward and forward with each call gives a ventriloquial quality to the sound.

A sun-warmed rock adjacent to a green meadow is the favorite lounging place for the **yellow-bellied marmot** (*Marmota flaviventris*). Spread out for a sunbath, the indolent, bushy-tailed marmot dozes as the diligent pika bustles nearby. Closely resembling the heavy-bodied, eastern woodchuck, this alpine relative is brown with a yellowish belly. Buff patches extend from below ears to shoulders. The face is darker than the back. Ears are small and round. With short legs and a fur coat that seems two sizes too big, the marmot makes a comic appearance as it shambles over boulders. Plants provide the diet of the marmot who eats all summer to

yellow-bellied marmot

fatten up for a long winter's sleep in a den dug under a rockpile.

The mountain marmot, also called rockchuck and yellow-footed marmot, lives in a colony and issues an alert with a chirp or whistle. It often stands upright with front feet against its chest in the manner of ground squirrels and chipmunks. Smaller than most raccoons, the marmot measures 18.5 to 27.5 inches from nose to end of tail. Less intimidated by humans than most wild creatures, the relaxed and curious marmot often remains on its rock to regard hikers and sometimes loiters on high mountain passes where it makes forthright appeals for tasty handouts.

A rock bright with red-orange jewel lichen identifies a **pika** or **marmot** perch. The extra nitrate from the animals' urine interacts with the rock to produce the vivid coloration of this plant. The pika's drying hay piles are another clue to its presence.

The forest is home to the slow, shuffling, solitary **porcupine** (*Erethizon dorsatum*). Primarily nocturnal, the porcupine may be sighted in early morning or in evening as it waddles, unhurried, away from intruders. At midday it might rest in an underground burrow, a hollow log, or a treetop. Protected by the 30,000 sharp quills on its rump and tail, this large woodland animal attracts few predators beyond the bobcat, who adroitly rolls it over to attack the vulnerable belly. Short legs support a chunky body with a high-arching back. Long yellowish guard hairs cover the porcupine's front half. The animal measures 25.5 to 36.5 inches from its nose to the tip of its dangerous tail. It is the stiff heavy tail which delivers pain and loosely-rooted, barbed quills to enemies. Many a dog returns to its owner bearing evidence of its naive meddling.

A vegetarian, the porcupine consumes plants in summer and cambium, the sweet inner bark of trees, in winter. Large irregular patches of bark stripped from tree trunks or branches give evidence for resident porcupines. Some trees are too damaged to survive. In May or June females bear a single very large offspring whose soft short quills harden a half hour after birth. North America has only one porcupine species.

Evidence of **beavers** (*Castor canadensis*) is common in valleys sculpted by mountain streams: conically shaped stumps; peeled logs and sticks; gnawed and felled trees; ponds and sloughs created by dams of woven reeds, saplings, and branches caulked with mud; dome-shaped lodges surrounded by water; and low scent mounds of grass, sticks, or mud built to mark territory. But though their handiwork is everywhere, the rodent engineers themselves are rarely seen by hikers. Nocturnal workers active all year, beavers are most often sighted in the evening by quiet, patient observers. Circumspect and alert, they slap black, flat, scaly tails against water to warn of danger. The distinctive tails also serve these good swimmers as rudders and are used as braces when beavers stand erect to gnaw on trees.

Beavers are the largest rodents in the Rockies, usually weighing 30 to 70 pounds and extending 35.5 to 48.0 inches in length. But beavers never stop growing, and some individuals may weigh in at 100 pounds. Now protected from overexploitation, wild beavers were once hunted to near-extinction for their soft, thick, dark brown fur. Large black hindfeet are webbed for swimming, and chestnut-colored front teeth, the beaver's tools, grow back if broken. When submerged, eyes are protected by clear membranes, and ears and nostrils are closed by valves. Beavers can remain underwater for 15 minutes because of specialized respiratory and cardiovascular systems. Aspens and willows are both building materials and food. Some bark is eaten immediately and the wood utilized. Other branches are stowed beneath the pond for winter consumption. Summer fare includes a variety of greens. Paired for life, beaver couples produce four or five well-furred kits in the spring. The young remain with their parents for two years before departing the home pond.

Hoofed Mammals

While sightings of mule deer are likely for most visitors, glimpses of the mountains' other hoofed creatures are restricted to dayhikers who venture beyond popular destinations. But the animals are there, and the excitement of discovering them lingers long after the event. Binoculars are helpful in observing elk, bighorn sheep, and mountain goats as their summer ranges are often inaccessible or distant.

Large, expressive, alert, and independently mobile, the ears of the **mule deer** (*Odocoileus hemionus*) give this animal its common name. Other characteristics include white rump and throat patches and tails white with black tips. Cinnamon summer coats become gray-brown in winter. Males' antlers branch equally with two main beams forking into two tines. Antlers can spread to four feet. The largest bucks may stand 3.5 feet at the shoulder and weigh 475 pounds. In mountain regions this western species migrates up and down to avoid heavy snows. In summer it is active in the early morning, in evening, and on moonlit nights.

Look for mule deer near valley streams, in high meadows, and at forest edges. Midday meetings are possible in wooded areas. When startled, mule deer move toward nearby tree cover with a stiff-legged, bounding gait. All four feet come down together. Bucks are usually solitary while single does are accompanied by their fawns or both fawns and yearlings. These small family groups space themselves widely to ensure adequate food and protective cover. Herbaceous plants and berries are summer forage. Mule deer often herd in winter and browse on the twigs of trees and shrubs.

The **elk** (*Cervus canadensis nelsoni*) may be the most majestic of the mountain mammals. Largest member of the deer family with exception of the moose, a mature bull elk may stand 5.0 feet at the shoulder and weigh 1000 pounds. Antlers of an adult are many tined with a main beam up to

5.0 feet long. The male grows a distinctive dark mane on its throat. All elk have thick necks, and both neck and underparts are darker than their tan backs. Rump and tail are a light yellowish-brown. The Rocky Mountain subspecies was given the name "wapiti" (white deer) by the Shawnee Indians because of its pale back, sides, and flanks.

Elk, while primarily nocturnal, are especially active at dusk and dawn. They graze in high open mountain pastures in summer. Most migrate to lower, wooded slopes in winter although bulls are occasionally seen above treeline. In the non-breeding season cows, calves, and juveniles herd separately from bulls. With a harem of up to 60 cows, the bull elk is the most polygamous deer in North America. His famous bugle, a call of dominance and challenge during the autumn rutting season, begins as a bellow, becomes a loud whistle or scream, and concludes with a series of grunts. All elk possess a repertoire of sounds.

Mule deer and their larger cousins, the **elk**, share many traits. In the autumn males use their racks of antlers in clashing battles for mates. Shed in winter, these bony weapons and symbols of sexuality grow back larger each summer. Females of both species lack antlers and are smaller and more delicately built than the males. One or two white-spotted young are born in the spring. Both species are good swimmers, migrate to lower elevations in winter, and are most visible early and late in the day. All deer have sharp front hooves which can strike swiftly and unexpectedly.

The handsome, muscular **bighorn sheep** (*Ovis canadensis*) favors habitats rarely disturbed by man. An excellent rock climber and strong jumper, it grazes alpine meadows near rocky cliffs. With hooves hard at the outer edge and spongy in the center, the bighorn has good traction in the treacherous places it wanders. The mountain sheep little resembles the domestic, woolly variety. Brown and smooth, the bighorn's coat is slightly longer and darker than that of a deer. Rump patch, muzzle, belly, and back of legs are white. Shed or snagged hair may identify bighorn trails, which are higher in elevation than deer trails and on less precipitous slopes than mountain goat trails. Both rams and ewes have horns, but while ewes wear small, backward-curving spikes, the rams carry massive, brown, curling headgear. As the ram ages, his C-shaped curl can grow to a full curl or beyond, and his horn spread may reach 33.0 inches. Never shed, the impressive horns are used in noisy, sometimes exhausting, butting contests with rivals during the fall mating season. A single lamb is born to a ewe in spring or early summer. Large rams stand 3.5 feet at the shoulder and weigh over 300 pounds.

Bighorns are gregarious, and in the spring mature rams band together while ewes and younger sheep form herds of about ten. In winter, when rams rejoin the others in their move to lower elevations, large herds of about 100 sheep are led by an old ewe. Active in daylight hours, the bighorn feeds in the early morning, midday, and evening. It is the only hoofed mammal in the mountains to bed down nightly in exactly the same spot, often for many years.

Perhaps the best representative of the aerial alpine world is the **mountain goat** (*Oreamnos americanus*). Trotting confidently across hairline ledges, this shaggy, white-haired mountaineer symbolizes the snowy, dangerous beauty of America's loftiest ranges. The mountain goat defies gravity in its high-altitude, vertical territory with the help of specialized hooves: two toes splay wide or grasp together to accommodate the terrain, and a rubbery sole provides traction on steep or smooth surfaces.

Actually a goat-antelope, related to the chamois of Europe and Asia Minor, the mountain goat differs from true goats: its dagger-like horns are not ridged or spiraled but smooth and only slightly curved; its beard is not chin hair but extension of a throat mane. Males can weigh 200 to 300 pounds. Females, or nannies, are smaller but are otherwise similar with black eyes, noses, horns, and hooves. Ears are erect and pointed, and tails are small. Short legs and powerful forequarters allow climbing and leaping feats. Heavy white coats have a thick fluffy underlayer covered by long, hollow, insulating guard hairs. Coats are shorter

mountain goat

112

in summer, and shed hair snagged on vegetation is evidence that goats are nearby.

Mountain goats can be seen at all hours but are usually active in morning and evening. Mature males tend to be solitary while females herd with other nannies, their kids, and juveniles. During the rut, or mating season, males threaten each other but, because of fragile skulls and horns, do not engage in head-bashing. They do, however, attempt to gore an opponent's flank. Accidental falls and golden eagle attacks claim some goats, but avalanches and rockslides cause the most fatalities. Mountain goats make only limited migrations up and down the slopes and feed on any available flower, grass, sedge, woody plant, lichen, or moss.

Birds

Fortunately for the dayhiker, most birds are not night-owls. And for the common species described here, binoculars are not required equipment.

A diminutive visitor to the mountains, the **broad-tailed hummingbird** (*Selasphorus platycercus*) is heard, if not seen, in lush, color-dotted meadows, in pinyon-juniper woodlands, in forests, in canyons, and in cultivated gardens. The male's unique feature is a loud musical trill made in flight. Wings with two pointed and separated primary outer feathers produce this unmistakable whirring sound. A glittering, rosy-red throat patch, the gorget, also distinguishes the male. Both sexes are 4.0 to 4.5 inches long and have

broad-tailed hummingbird

metallic green backs and crowns, white chests, gray underparts, rounded tails, and long, narrow, black bills. Flower nectar and tiny insects constitute the diet of broad-tails. They faithfully return to nest on the same branch in the same tree year after year.

Smaller than the broad-tail and summering in Alaska and the Yukon, the **rufous hummingbird** (*Selasphorus rufous*) migrates through Colorado, lingering on its way to Latin America. Females of both species are similar, with the rufous having some rusty color on sides and underparts. Males differ, with the rufous wearing bronze-green crowns, rusty backs, and orange-red gorgets. Rufous hummingbirds of both sexes are ferocious in defending feeding sites. Perching nearby, they attack intruders with an angry buzz. The aerial battles provide a lively spectacle for humans.

All hummingbirds have remarkable speed and can dive, hover, fly forward, backward, and upward. But they cannot glide or walk. Resting heartbeat is about 500 beats per minute. They consume half their weight in sugar each day, licking nectar from tubular flowers with their long tongues. They are important as pollinators. The female seeks out a male in his territory, but after mating, she raises her two young alone. Males' courting behavior involves fast fancy flying. Hummers have no down feathers for warmth and may conserve energy at night by inducing a state of torpidity—a rapid lowering of metabolism and body temperature that leaves the birds in temporary suspended animation, defenseless and nonfunctional. By September, cold nights and a dwindling supply of flowers drive the hummingbirds from the Rockies to tropical regions.

Compared to the hummingbird, the **black-billed magpie** (*Pica pica*) is a giant. At a length of 17.5 to 22.0 inches, the bird is conspicuous for its size, its extremely long tail, and its dramatic black and white feathers. A crow relative, the handsome magpie has a black bill, head, breast, and underparts. A blue-green iridescence colors wings and tail. Its belly, shoulders, and primary wing feathers are white. Not a bird of the tundra, the black-billed magpie resides year-round in the montane zone in brush-covered areas, in woods, or in streamside growth. Social creatures after breeding, magpies often feed together and flock to adjacent treetops at dusk. Nests are sturdy, bulky, domed constructions where six to nine blotched, greenish eggs are hatched. The bird's nasal voice calls "mag? mag? mag?" or "yak yak yak". Like the crow, the magpie is an adept scavenger and can often be seen patrolling roadsides.

black-billed magpie

The bright flash of turquoise darting from a tree or hovering near the ground scouting for insects is the **mountain bluebird** (*Sialia currucoides*), smallest of the Rockies' several blue-hued birds. The bluebird, a member of the thrush family, prefers open areas interrupted by a few trees. It nests in a tree cavity in montane woodlands and in subalpine forests near meadows. The male bird's breast is a lighter blue than his back, and his belly is white. Less conspicuous, the female is gray-brown with a trace of blue on wings, rump, and tail. The bluebird moves to lower elevations and the southern part of its range in winter.

gray jay

The beautiful mountain bluebird is only 6.5 to 8.0 inches in length, making it easy to distinguish from the much larger, midnight-blue **Steller's jay** (*Cyanocitta stelleri macrolopha*) that shares its territory. Steller's jay extends 12.0 to 13.5 inches, and its dark head and crest are its best identification. Look for it in the tops of coniferous trees where it prefers to nest. It may also survey tundra regions and places where humans pause to camp or eat. Like its crow relations, its voice is harsh, and it does not migrate.

Bolder and greedier than its blue cousin, the **gray jay** (*Perisoreus canadensis capitalis*) is familiar to anyone who carries food on expeditions through coniferous mountain forests. Popularly called the camp robber, the gray jay is also known as Canada jay or whiskey jack. It stores much of the food that it appropriates by hiding it high among needles of trees. Like other jays, this bird is fairly large at 10.0 to 13.0 inches from bill to tail. Its back and tail are dark gray, and its nape, bill, and legs are black. Face, breast, and underparts are nearly white. **Clark's nutcracker** (*Nucifraga columbiana*), another mountain bird of similar size and coloration, has a long, pointed bill and lacks a black nape patch. Both birds are in the crow family, beg shamelessly for handouts, often incubate eggs before the last snow has fallen, and do not migrate. Nesting below treelimit, they may cruise over alpine areas scanning for food.

Like the mountain goat among hoofed animals, the **white-tailed ptarmigan** (*Lagopus leucurus altipetens*) among birds is most symbolic of the intensely beautiful land above the trees. And like the goat, this special high-alpine grouse matches the snow that isolates high meadows and rocky tundra for eight to ten months of each year. Pure white in winter except for black bill and eyes, the plump ptarmigan wears mottled brown feathers on its head, breast, and back as camouflage during the brief summer. It nests on the ground, remains so motionless, and blends so perfectly with its surroundings that a passing hiker may miss it entirely.

The white-tailed ptarmigan at 12.0 to 13.0 inches is about the size of a small chicken. It prefers running to flying and communicates with soft low hoots and clucks. The male ptarmigan is the only bird to remain on the tundra all year. Nestled in the snow in a group, individual birds loose little body heat.

white-tailed ptarmigan

Feet and legs are heavily feathered for warmth, and the feathers transform feet into snowshoes. Female birds retreat to willow thickets below treelimit until mating in May. Though pairs bond for life, their only contact is during the breeding season, and females raise chicks alone. Summer snows, predator birds, and weasels are dangerous to exposed eggs.

Wildflowers

"Flowers are the beautiful hieroglyphics of nature, with which she indicates how much she loves us."

—Goethe

Wildflowers

MANY HIKERS TAKE TO THE TRAILS FOR THE LARGENESS OF THE SCENERY—towering pinnacles, craggy summits, vast basins—and then find themselves lingering over the smallest things in the landscape. And for others, what might have begun as a purely physical endeavor becomes, quite without design, a search for the most fragrant columbine, the bluest harebell, the tallest monkshood, the most diminutive forget-me-not, or the first arctic gentian of the season. Delicate and evanescent, these wildflowers have a subtle, seductive charm.

The central and southern Rocky Mountains nurture a greater variety of plants than do mountain ranges in North America's east and far west. The geology of the region has encouraged such diversity, providing almost limitless subject matter for painters and photographers and giving the challenge of identification and the pleasure of discovery to botanists and amateur naturalists.

Unlike flowers blooming elsewhere, mountain wildflowers must endure, even in midsummer, great extremes in weather. Additionally, they are subjected to strong ultraviolet radiation. And they must mature in a curtailed growing season. To flourish as they so obviously do, Rocky Mountain wildflowers have made remarkable adaptations.

Most beginning naturalists focus on flower identification, a task of enough complexity and confusion to occupy countless summers. Many field guides group wildflowers by color, their most obvious characteristic. Such organization is very helpful and, paired with flower shape, quickly limits choices in the identification process.

A parallel approach is compatible with walking a trail through the many environments of the mountains. As you hike, you travel through places dry and damp, shaded and bright, sheltered and windswept. You also move from one elevation to another—from one life zone to the one above or below. The combination of local conditions and altitude determines which wildflowers you are likely to encounter. If you see brookcress along one cold, subalpine stream, for example, you can look for it along the next.

The environments covered by the longest hikes may vary from the hot, parched, brushy slopes of the lower montane zone near Aspen to cold, windy passes on alpine tundra. During an ascent to a pass or a peak, hikers progress from low sagebrush-juniper regions to the aspen groves and mixed aspen-evergreen woodlands of the mid and upper montane; they pass through cool subalpine forests of spruce and fir into high meadows where wildflowers multiply as trees diminish in size and number. From these subalpine meadows, some lush and wet with snowmelt streams, trails mount to treeless tundra. But even in this harsh, dry, unforgiving place, exquisite alpine flowers persist.

Sagebrush Slopes

The sunny, gravelly hillsides around Aspen and Snowmass are dotted with big sagebrush, a large silvery gray-green variety. The shrub's flashy orange-red companion is **Wyoming** or **narrowleaf paintbrush**, a parasitic flower drawing nourishment from its sagebrush host. The petals of all paint-brushes are inconspicuous and green while the upturned bracts, actually modified leaves, at the stem's top give the plant its brilliance. Narrowleaf paintbrush has very slender colored bracts and is Wyoming's state flower. It stands 8.0 to 20.0 inches tall.

Other species of paintbrush grow at higher elevations and in different soil compositions. They may be yellow, cream, scarlet, or rose. Paintbrush species are difficult to identify as they tend to hybridize. A cream flower with purple streaks is a hybrid found in meadows high in the Elk Mountains.

A white bell-shaped flower, looking something like a frail tulip, also favors these dry sagebrush slopes. The showy, three-petaled **sego lily** stands erect on almost leafless, usually unbranched stems. The inside base of the flower is gold, fringed, and marked with purple. The sego lily is occasionally a pale lilac hue. Its slender stems are 6.0 to 18.0 inches tall, and

sego lily

119

its flowerhead is 1.0 to 2.0 inches across. This white lily is Utah's state flower, and its bulb was eaten by the Ute Indians and starving Mormon settlers. A similar species growing elsewhere in the west is pink to magenta in color. Both flowers are sometimes called mariposa tulip or mariposa lily.

Fremont's geranium, a wild pink species, is another common resident of the sagebrush environment and of the dry meadows of higher elevation. The one-inch flowerheads have five rounded petals with purplish veins. They top graceful branching stems of 12.0 to 24.0 inches. A taller, closely-related species, **Richardson's geranium**, is white or pale pink and grows among the aspens. Leaves are five-lobed on long stalks.

Aspen Woods

The gentle filtered light of aspen groves allows many plants to flourish among the grasses. Brightening the woods is **heartleaf arnica**, a member of the sunflower family. Two to three pairs of opposite, heart-shaped leaves grow beneath one or more flowerheads. Blossoms are up to 3.5 inches across with 10 to 15 yellow rays around centers of tiny yellow disk flowers. The tips of the ray petals have shallow notches. Arnica blossoms are composites—two kinds of flowers in one head—like any sunflower or daisy. Stems are hairy and grow 8.0 to 20.0 inches. Plants never crowd but space themselves about the woods. Heartleaf arnica also adds cheerful spots of brightness to deep conifer forests.

Yellow composites are plentiful in the mountains. Such plants share so many characteristics that identification of a particular genus or species is a frustrating exercise. There are, for instance, 12 species of arnica in the Rockies.

Flowering nearby is another composite, the lavender **aspen daisy** or **showy daisy**. Its most important characteristic is the double row of many fine narrow rays surrounding its flat yellow center. The stem supports several two-inch flowerheads and is clasped by smooth lance-shaped leaves. The plant is 12.0 to 36.0 inches high. In mid- and late summer these pretty daisies mass in great numbers in wet aspen woods and in damp meadows near woods.

Cow parsnip, one of the real giants among wildflowers, favors moist, lightly-shaded woods and bogs. This stout member of the carrot-parsley family grows 3.0 to 7.0 feet in height in the mountains and bears a flat-topped, lacy flowerhead 6.0 to 12.0 inches across. The white umbrella-like flower clusters are borne on a thick, hollow, hairy stem. Huge leaves are divided into three large leaflets with toothed edges. They are somewhat maple-like. The plant's close cousin, lacy white **giant angelica**, likes the same damp environment. It is memorable for its large spherical flower clusters that resemble fuzzy softballs or gigantic dandelion puffs.

cow parsnip

Conifer Forests

The acid soil and the deep shade of an evergreen forest with its cone-bearing pines, firs, and spruces discourages the growth of wildflowers. But a few plants, including arnica, are well-adapted to the life under the big trees, and a variety bloom in sunny clearings or at forest edges. **Jacob's ladder** often flowers under spruces within sight of a meadow. It forms a loose clump of leafy branching stems that terminate in a cluster of light blue flowers. Five round petals encircle a white and yellow center. Tiny oval leaflets on opposite sides of the plants' leaf stems contribute to a ladder-like appearance. The plant is no more than 6.0 to 8.0 inches tall and can sometimes be found in protected spots above treeline.

Even less conspicuous than dainty Jacob's ladder is the tiny **wood nymph** or **shy maiden**. Easily overlooked, the modest white flower holds its face to the earth. The

wood nymph

121

nodding waxy blossoms are star-like. Five spreading petals encircle a prominent, round, green ovary—the organ in which seeds develop. Flowers are solitary on a 2.0- to 8.0-inch stem. Several rounded leaves ring the plant's base. The fragrant wood nymph is hidden like treasure in wet mossy areas of cool forests.

Streams and Bogs

Brookcress or **bittercress** is so fond of cold running water that its roots sometimes extend into the streams themselves. Blooming in white clusters atop leafy stems, this plant bears the characteristic four-petaled flower of the mustard family to which it belongs. Individual blooms are 1.0 to 1.5 inches across, and the shiny green leaves are somewhat heart-shaped. Brookcress usually stands 10.0 to 30.0 inches in height.

A taller plant and a neighbor to brookcress in marshy meadows and on montane and subalpine streambanks is graceful **chimingbells** or **mertensia**. Its many blue flowers dangle in loose clusters from its upper stem, sometimes causing the whole plant to dip. The narrow bell-like blossoms develop from pink buds. The elongated leaves are numerous. A short version grows on alpine tundra, one of many species in the Rockies. Chimingbells goes by other names: mountain bluebells, languid lady, Virginia bluebells, lungwort, and cowslip.

Parry's primrose clamors for attention with its intense magenta blossoms. It is a favorite with hikers despite its carrion odor. Five rounded petals, notched at the tip, surround a bright yellow eye. Several of the glowing, reddish-purple flowerheads crown a stout, leafless stalk about 6.0 to 12.0 inches high. Oblong, fleshy leaves stand erect at the base of the plant.

Parry's primrose

Sometimes the primrose sprouts from a small knoll in a subalpine stream. It grows at elevations over 10,000 feet and survives in protected rock crevices and wet sites across alpine tundra.

High Dry Meadows

For many dayhikers the best part of any trip is the time spent in the meadows of the mountains' upper valleys. These high open places permit widening vistas as dense continuous forest is left behind. Trees occur in isolated stands, often dividing one field from another. In the most exposed high meadows, soil is dry from strong sun and relentless wind. Grasses grow in tight clumps, and the wildflowers that color these fields are largely perennials with well-established roots. Though plant cover is not exceptionally dense in dry meadows, many lovely flowers persevere.

mountain harebell

The **mountain harebell** or **common harebell** is abundant and widespread, flourishing in dry places low and high. It is much loved for its fragile beauty. One or more blue nodding flowers hang from slender stems bearing fine, grasslike leaves. The bell-shaped flowerheads extend about one inch and have five pointed lobes curving gently backward. The small round leaves that nestle at the stem's base often wither before the bells bloom. The mountain harebell can be dwarfed or tall, but its height is usually 6.0 to 18.0 inches. This flower is also known as witches' thimble and bluebell of Scotland.

A blazing comrade of the quiet harebell is **scarlet gilia**, also popularly known as **fairy trumpet** or **skyrocket**. Its various names accurately characterize the flower's appearance. The brilliant red "trumpets" are 1.0 to 1.5 inches long with five pointed lobes bent sharply backward. They grow singly or in small clusters from a nearly leafless stem. Lower leaves are fern-like. Scarlet gila stands 12.0 to 18.0 inches and exudes a skunk-like smell when crushed. Its nectar is a favorite of hummingbirds. The flower has additional names: desert trumpet, skunk flower, and polecat plant.

Yarrow is a hearty, adaptable plant, thriving in poor soil at all elevations. It likes low sagebrush slopes and is conspicuous in the high dry meadows near treeline. It makes appearances in woods and on tundra. Yarrow's flattish cluster of small dull-white flowerheads caps a fibrous stem bearing feathery, fern-like leaves. The slightly woolly plant is 12 to 20 inches tall. Yarrow was supposedly used by Achilles to treat his soldiers' wounds. The Ute Indians of the Elk Mountains also employed yarrow as a medicinal, and early white settlers found it helpful for nosebleeds.

High Wet Meadows

Even more delightful than dry meadows are the damp places high in the mountains nourished by melting snow and by outflow from alpine lakes. The water may be a rivulet, brook, stream, or creek. But whatever its name, it is life-giving. Such luxuriant places, though subjected to extreme cold most of the year, may be protected from wind by a fringe of trees or a ridge of stone. High wet mountain meadows are among the earth's loveliest natural gardens.

The spreading growth of grasses in the moist meadow paints a dense, flattering background for stunning masses of purple lupine and rosy paintbrush and for artfully mixed floral bouquets of yellow, crimson, white, violet, and pink. Wildflowers are in each hollow, on each hillock. They soften the severe landscape, transforming it into a gentle sanctuary. To lovers of flowers, the soaring skyline is but a backdrop to the splendor underfoot.

Brookcress and chimingbells are here, of course, as their range extends from wet locales in the montane zone through subalpine heights. And Parry's primrose is right at home. But these elevated sunny and soggy valleys over 10,000 feet are carpeted by countless handsome flower species. Two that catch the eye, and sometimes cause confusion, are **king's crown**, shaded deep red to maroon or burgundy, and **queen's crown**, also named **rose crown** for its coloration.

Both plants have tiny flowers, each with five sharply-pointed petals, crowded together at the top of an unbranched stem. Both plants' stems bear many short, smooth, succulent leaves. But king's crown flowerheads are somewhat flattened while queen's crown heads are round to egg-shaped. King's crown blooms from late spring to midsummer while queen's crown begins its show at high season. The brief period of overlap allows for helpful comparison. King's crown rarely exceeds 6.0 inches in height while queen's crown can grow to 12.0 inches. And, finally, though both plants range onto tundra, deep red king's crown ventures into rocky areas while pink-hued queen's crown sticks closer to streams and may extend to lower elevations than its mate.

Blooming in mid- to late summer is the elegant **explorer's gentian** or **bog gentian**, surely the jewel of damp meadows. Its appearance gives August hikes an added mission.

explorer's gentian

Deep sapphire-blue upright bells are large and solitary on the stem, distinguishing explorer's from numerous other gentian species flowering in the Elk Mountains. These single, cup-like blooms are about 1.5 inches tall and have five rounded petal lobes separated by two tiny sharp teeth. Insides are striped or speckled and colored a pale greenish-yellow. Stems 2.0 to 10.0 inches tall support pairs of leaves that are oval, smooth, and opposite.

Bobbing at tops of slender stems everywhere across moist high meadows and alpine tundra is ubiquitous **American bistort** or **western bistort**. Looking like puffs of cotton, the dense heads are comprised of many tiny white to pinkish flowers. Smooth stems have swollen knobs like bamboo, are tinged with red, and exhibit a few grass-like leaves. Larger oblong leaves grow at the plant's base from the thick edible root. Flower clusters are 1.0 to 2.0 inches long and plants are 8.0 to 20.0 inches tall.

Bistort, a member of the buckwheat family is often confused with **snowball saxifrage**, also called **diamond leaf saxifrage**, with which it shares territory. But snowball saxifrage is a shorter plant with a leafless, thick, and slightly fuzzy stem. Its flowerhead is white to cream. And its thick basal leaves have blunt teeth. Snowball saxifrage appears in fewer numbers than bistort and has many closely-related, even less-common, relatives.

Snowbeds

Many hikes go around or over snowbeds, or snowfields, at midsummer. There is an interesting variety in this for both the physical experience and for the visual one. A snowbed is more than a slippery obstacle across a trail; it is a micro-environment with specialized plant life. One of the most humble of these plants is a minute green alga encased in a rose-red gelatinous coat. The red pigmentation may protect the alga from radiation damage, but to hikers passing by, it is more appreciated for the water-melon-pink coloring it imparts to the snow.

A close look at the snowbed's periphery is an introduction to robust flowers, seemingly oblivious to cold.

Snow buttercups are aptly named as they sometimes poke through the retreating edges of a drift. They have been discovered with half-open blossoms many feet beneath the surface. Their five broad petals are a bright shiny yellow, and leaves are finely divided in six threadlike segments at the bottom of a sturdy stem 4.0 to 8.0 inches tall. One to three blooms, each three-quarters of an inch wide, grow atop the stem. The flower is closely related to, and possibly a variation of, **alpine buttercup**. The latter is oversize, the largest flowerhead of its type in North America. Blossoms may be 1.5 inches wide. This big buttercup favors a similar cold wet habitat and bears one to three flowers per plant. Three-lobed leaves are glossy and basal.

The brilliant yellow **glacier lily** sometimes thrusts its pair of smooth, lance-shaped leaves up through the snow. The 4.0 to 8.0-inch leaves flank one or two stems supporting single flowers. These sophisticated lilies have six petal-like segments that arch gracefully

marsh marigolds

backward. Long stamens project downward from inside the drooping flowerhead. Glacier lilies stand 6.0 to 12.0 inches tall and are found only west of the Continental Divide. Bears dig for the tasty bulbs. This wild-flower is also known as snowlily, avalanche lily, and dogtooth violet.

126

Marsh marigolds are impossible to ignore. They are abundant in boggy spots throughout the subalpine and alpine regions. Impatient to bloom, these low plants push through snow and blanket ground still partially submerged in spring runoff. They flower when night temperatures are below zero. Their broad, bowl-shaped blossoms have prominent yellow centers surrounded by 6 to 12 waxy, white, petal-like sepals. The flower may wear a lavender-tinged exterior. Blooms are up to 2.0 inches across and are alone on a short stem. The large waxy leaves of the marsh marigold are heart-shaped with lightly scalloped edges. They radiate on stalks from the plant's base. Marsh marigolds stand 3.0 to 8.0 inches tall. This member of the buttercup family also goes by elk's lip and cowslip.

Alpine Tundra

alpine sunflower

While snow lingers in protected subalpine meadows, creating marshes well into summer, spring arrives on alpine tundra and on exposed meadows just below treeline. Wind scours the peaks and unguarded slopes, driving away snow and eroding the soil. So above the trees, as in some lower regions, plants send forth strong roots to search for nutrients and moisture.

Alpine plants make other adaptations to their cold windy world by clinging near the ground in mats or cushions; by growing fine hairs for warming insulation, for diffusion of intense sunlight, and for reduction of water loss; by stockpiling energy with years of quiescence; or by sending forth over-size, ostentatious blossoms to lure necessary pollinators.

The biggest, brightest, and possibly the woolliest of these is **alpine sunflower**, also identified as **rydbergia** or **old man of the mountain**. Large golden heads glow atop short stout stems. Twenty or more showy rays with three-lobed tips surround the broad golden disk of this composite. Flowerheads are 2.0 to 4.0 inches across. Long soft hairs make a dense silvery-gray covering for stems, feathery leaves, and bracts—the green overlapping scales at the flower's back. Alpine sunflower spends years developing its taproot and its leaves before dazzling with its first and final show. This sunflower faithfully faces east, providing a natural compass for alpine hikers.

Conspicuous, unique, and easily identifiable, **purple fringe** or **silky phacelia** likes the open rocky places and gravelly soils of the subalpine and tundra life zones. Erect stems support elongated compact clusters of purple flowers. The soft fringed look of the flowerhead is produced by long delicate projections, called stamens, which emerge from the center of each tiny flower in the large cluster. The yellow tip of each stamen holds the plant's pollen. Long silky hairs give a silver cast to the dissected, almost fern-like leaves. Purple fringe spikes grow in a clump and stand 8.0 to 12.0 inches high.

The discovery of minute blue **alpine forget-me-nots** at the crest of a mountain pass brings flower enthusiasts to their knees in wonder and delight. Hugging the ground atop a tight cushion of small tufted leaves are simple, precious, fragrant flowers only one-quarter inch in diameter. Five round petals, fused in a tube at their base, open widely to encircle a bright yellow eye. Occasional flowers are white, but most are delicate to deep blue. Alpine forget-me-nots are protected from the cold by their low growth habit, their furry leaves, and anthocyanin, a pigment that converts light to heat and gives the flowers their intense, memorable blue.

Colorado blue columbine

No introduction to mountain wildflowers would be whole without inclusion of the **Colorado blue columbine**, the state flower since 1899. Though familiar through countless photographs, the real thing is still a delight. Yellow stamens at center are surrounded by five light blue to white petals which extend backward into long blue spurs containing the flower's nectar. A ring of five blue, pointed, petal-like sepals frames the white. The spurs, up to 2.0 inches in length, are the flower's primary characteristic.

Colorado blue columbine can be deep sky blue to nearly white. It blooms from aspen woods to above treeline. Its perfume is enchanting.

Images of the exquisite columbine are everywhere, and once, the flowers themselves were abundant. But the public's fondness for the fragrant wildflower led to indiscriminate picking and digging, extinguishing many original sites. Conservation efforts of the Colorado Mountain Club resulted in a 1925 state law protecting the columbine. In 1971 a broader statute was enacted that forbids destruction of any natural plant growth on state land.

The National Forest Service supervises federal forests and wilderness areas. Its regulations prohibit damage to and removal of plants classified as "threatened, endangered, sensitive, rare, or unique". And its regulations require a special use permit for action impacting all non-classified plant life. Fines for violations range from fifty to five-hundred dollars.

With more recreational use of forest and wilderness, more unenlightened people threaten rare and endangered flowers. But few mountain wildflowers will transplant to other environments as they have evolved into specialized, high-altitude life forms. And picking any flower halts its reproduction by stopping its seed production. Leave nature's jewels where they grow and their descendents will charm you when you next return.

Never pick or dig wildflowers on public land.

Flower Guide

Common Name	Locale	Color	Height	Distinctive Characteristic
Wyoming paintbrush	dry sunny slope	orange-red	8"-20"	head like end of artist's brush
sego lily	dry sunny slope	white	6"-18"	3 petals; gold & purple interior; tulip shape; slender stem
Fremont's geranium	dry sunny slope	pink	12"-24"	5 rounded petals w/ purple veins
Richardson's geranium	aspen woods	white	18"-32"	5 rounded petals w/ purple veins
heartleaf arnica	wooded areas	yellow	8"-20"	heart-shaped leaves in opposite pairs; broad composite; hairy stem
aspen daisy	aspen woods	lavender	12"-36"	many narrow rays around yellow disk; leaves clasp stem
cow parsnip	woods or bog	white	36"-84"	6"-12" lacy, flat-topped flowerhead
giant angelica	woods or bog	white	36"-84"	3"-6" flowerhead like fluffy softball
Jacob's ladder	conifer forest	light blue	6"-8"	small, oval, opposite leaves along stem; small clusters of flowers
wood nymph	damp forest	white	2"-8"	solitary star-like flower facing down
brookcress	stream or bog	white	10"-30"	4 petals; grow in clusters at top
chimingbells	stream or bog	blue	20"-48"	clusters of dangling narrow bells
Parry's primrose	stream or bog	red-purple	6"-12"	5 notched petals; yellow eye; stout stem; above 10,000 feet

Common Name	Locale	Color	Height	Distinctive Characteristic
mountain harebell	dry areas	blue	6"-18"	bell dangling from slender stem
scarlet gilia	high dry meadow	scarlet	12"-18"	blazing red color; trumpet shape
yarrow	nearly all	white	12"-20"	flat head; feathery fern-like leaves
king's crown	high wet meadow	maroon	4"-6"	flatish head and succulent leaves
queen's crown	high wet meadow	rose pink	6"-12"	rounded head and succulent leaves
explorer's gentian	high wet meadow	blue	2"-10"	large upright bell solitary on stem
American bistort	high wet meadow	white	8"-20"	one-inch puffball on slender stem
snowball saxifrage	high wet meadow	white	2"-12"	one-inch puffball on thick fuzzy stem
snow buttercup	snowbed	yellow	4"-8"	5 shiny petals; 3/4" across; finely divided leaves
alpine buttercup	snowbed	yellow	4"-8"	5 shiny petals; 1" to 1.5" across; basal, lobed leaves
glacier lily	snowbed	yellow	6"-12"	6 segments arched backward; 2 lance-like leaves at base
marsh marigold	snowbed or high wet meadow	white	3"-8"	6-12 petals; bowl-shaped head; large basal heart-shaped leaves
alpine sunflower	alpine tundra	yellow	3"-10"	20 or more notched rays; 2"-4" wide; long , soft hairs on back, stem, leaves; faces east
purple fringe	alpine tundra	purple	8"-12"	soft, elongated cluster of tiny flowers
alpine forget-me-nots	alpine tundra	blue	1"-3"	5 round petals; yellow eye; 1/4" wide; grow in low clumps
blue columbine	aspens to tundra	blue & white	12"-24"	5 petals ending in long blue spurs

131

WILD-
FLOWERS

Trees

"*What we love, when on a summer day we step into the coolness of a wood, is that its boughs close up behind us. We are escaped, into another room of life.*"

—Donald Culross Peattie

Trees

MOUNTAIN WILDLIFE CAN BE ELUSIVE, AND WILDFLOWERS, EPHEMERAL. But unless felled by logger, avalanche, or fire, the trees remain reassuringly permanent. In time, aspens sharing spaces with pines or firs will be eclipsed by the slowly-maturing big conifers, but this is an unhurried process. So the trees stand, offering homes and sustenance to woodland habitants and shelter, shade and scent to human transients.

Elevation, moisture, and a slope's orientation to the sun determine which trees will succeed. Aspen and Snowmass are located in the montane zone which, in central Colorado, has forests of Douglas fir, white fir, Colorado blue spruce, and quaking aspen. On dry warm hillsides grow the small oaks and junipers common to the lower foothills zone. High on cold north-facing slopes of the montane appear the Englemann spruces and subalpine firs which dominate the transitional subalpine life zone. Above 11,500 feet, in the windswept region called alpine tundra, lies a high altitude desert bereft of trees. With a few basic facts and awareness of elevation, visitors to the mountains can easily identify several native trees.

Many leafy deciduous trees in the Rockies are variations on familiar varieties found elsewhere. Generally, the mountain versions are more diminutive, sometimes no more than shrubs. The extremes of high altitude and/or a paucity of moisture reduce tree size. Colorado has a multitude of small willow species, and many hikers know them as the thickets of interlocking bushes that blanket damp valleys, sometimes obscuring trails. Other willows are minute tundra plants requiring a hand lens for inspection. Oaks are hardly mighty in the mountains but are, instead, contorted small trees often clustered in groves with an understory of serviceberry or sagebrush.

Aspens, however, so emblematic of this particular place, are unmistakably themselves. Trees of the mountains and northern climes, the lithe, graceful aspens inspire essays and beautiful, moody photographs. Suffused as

Aspen is with images of aspens, there remains, for all that, a quiet allure, perhaps an enchantment, and certainly a sweet soft melody to the real thing.

The **quaking aspen** *(Populus tremuloides)*, also commonly called the trembling aspen or golden aspen, is named for its leaves which quiver and dance with every whiff of breeze. Flattened at right angles to the leaves, long stalks act as pivots. The mellifluous fluttering of an aspen grove is calming, almost hypnotic. Like the cottonwood, the aspen is a poplar. Its thin green leaves are nearly round with a short point—a shape something like a plump heart. Edges are gently toothed, and undersides are pale. Bark is thin, soft, white, and lightly powdered to protect against the intense ultraviolet of high altitude. Native Americans once applied this dusty sunscreen to their own skins. The tree prunes itself, leaving dark eye-shaped marks where limbs once grew. In the west, aspens propagate asexually by root sprouts, cloning themselves by the thousands. Arising from the root of a single tree, a grove is technically one giant organism. Aspens often grow in pure stands, making more dazzling their gilded autumn dress.

Aspens are intolerant of shade, and saplings survive only at the bright edges of a grove. Lifespan of a tree is less than a hundred years, and the wood, usually defiled by heart-rot fungi, is not prized by lumbermen. But flora and fauna prosper in the airy groves, and we humans find inspiration in the aspens' melodies and seasonal transmutations.

There is no blazing raiment, no frivolous dancing, no tremulous voice for the **conifers**. Dignified and imperturbable, spired and sturdy, these ever-greens mimic the enduring vertical landscape. Cone-bearing trees fall into four categories: pine, fir, spruce, and juniper. Needles, rich with resin that acts as antifreeze, are decidedly different for each. A quick, close-up look or touch will discriminate.

Pines' needles grow in clusters, or bundles, of two to five needles per cluster. The lodgepole pine species of the Rockies has cones that open to drop their seeds only when heated, making it a pioneer tree in burned areas. Pinyons produce the delicious "pine nuts" used in pesto sauce, salads, and cookies. Bristlecone pines are possibly the oldest known living things on earth and have been dated to more than 4600 years old in

California. They and limber pines sometimes survive in bent, stunted, shrublike form, called "krummholz", in the lee of rocks at 12,000 feet.

Firs are considered "friendly" trees because of their flat, flexible, blunt-tipped needles. Fir needles grow singly, not in bundles. Subalpine firs and their companions, Englemann spruces, take krummholz form at treelimit.

Spruces also produce separate, unbunched, needles. But spruce needles are stiff and prickly, not soft and feathery. And spruce needles are four-sided, easily rolled between two fingers. The Colorado blue spruce is the state tree and prefers moist, cool locations.

Tree	Needle Characteristics
Pine	grow in clusters of two to five
Fir	grow singly, flat, flexible, blunt-tipped
Spruce	grow singly, four-sided, stiff, sharp

A tree's silhouette, branch arrangement, height, cones, bark, color, and local environment help in identifying one species of pine, fir, or spruce from another within the Rocky Mountain region.

Junipers come in two quite different forms in the mountains. The common juniper (*Juniperus communis*) is a bristly, prostrate shrub with very sharp short needles. Its "cones" are berries that mature from a pale frosted green to dark blue. It is tolerant of many growing conditions.

The Rocky Mountain juniper, sometimes called a cedar, is a pyramid-shaped evergreen of small to medium-size. Its "needles" are like tiny, overlapping, pointed scales wrapped around its branches. Its cones resemble whitish-blue berries. This juniper (*Juniperus scopulorum*) is often found with pinyon pines and is closely related to the eastern red cedar.

136

Glossary

Glossary

alpine	pertaining to a high-elevation mountain region above continuous forest
anthocyanin	red, blue, or violet pigments in the cell-sap of plants
basal	originating from and clustered at the base of a plant's stem
bract	a modified leaf, often small and scalelike, sometimes large and colorful, at base of flower or on its stalk
cairn	a pile of rocks deliberately stacked to serve as a trail marker
carbohydrates	organic compounds in foods, primarily sugars and starches, that deliver energy to working muscles
composite	one blossom composed of two individual flower types, such as ray and disk flowers in a daisy, aster, or sunflower
conifers	cone-bearing trees, including spruces, firs, pines, larches, hemlocks; all with needle-like leaves
deciduous	shedding leaves annually at a certain season
dehydration	a condition in which the body has insufficient water to function normally
disk flowers	tiny tubular flowers at center of a composite, such as a daisy
evergreen	a tree or plant that remains green throughout the winter
family	a group of related genera, such as composite flowers or deer or willows

ford   a shallow place where a stream or river may be crossed by walking or by riding on horseback

genus   category of plant or animal classification smaller than a family and larger than a species; consists of one or more closely-related species

giardia   a parasitic organism found in mountain streams and lakes that is responsible for acute intestinal distress

glycogen   the form in which the liver and muscles store carbohydrates

high altitude cerebral edema   swelling of brain tissue at high elevation caused by increased blood flow and accumulation of fluid; a serious manifestation of acute mountain sickness

high altitude pulmonary edema   swelling caused by accumulation of fluid within lung tissue; experienced most often by those who climb rapidly to high elevation, heavy smokers, or those with pre-existing lung problems; a serious manifestation of acute mountain sickness

hybrid   product of fertilization by another species or variety within a species; usually displaying traits of both parents

hypothermia   a dangerous decrease in the temperature of the body's inner core; caused by cold, wetness, or wind

krummholz   environmentally-dwarfed trees growing at treeline

lug sole   a shoe or boot sole with many blocky projections for holding fast to uneven surfaces

montane   pertaining to the mountain area between the foothills and subalpine zones; a region with a diversity of life forms

mountain sickness   collection of symptoms produced by decreased oxygen at high altitude; includes headache, nausea, breathlessness, sleeplessness, and loss of appetite

ovary	the seed-producing part of the pistil in flowering plants
perennial	a plant that lives three seasons or more
peripheral edema	painless swelling of face, hands, ankles, or feet caused by high altitude and/or exercise
pistil	the female reproductive organ of a flower
pollen	male reproductive cells produced by the stamens
ray flowers	strap-shaped petals surrounding the disk in a composite flower
rut	the period of sexual excitement of male hoofed mammals; the fall mating season of deer, sheep, and goats
saddle	a dip or low point in a ridge, often between two peaks
scree	accumulation of rock fragments of softball size or smaller
sepals	small, usually green leaves outside the petals; sometimes colored as in columbines and marsh marigolds
snowbed snowfield	an expanse of snow persisting to midsummer and nourishing distinct plant species
species	a related group of individual plants or animals that interbreed and produce similar offspring
spur	a slender, often hollow projection from a flower part
stamen	the male, or pollen-producing, organ of a flower
subalpine	pertaining to the high-altitude transitional zone where large trees diminish in size and number; between montane and alpine zones
talus	accumulation of unstable rock fragments smaller than boulders below steep slopes or cliffs; sorted by gravity with largest at bottom

tarn a pond filling a glacially-scoured rock depression above treeline

treelimit highest elevation at which trees can survive;
treeline approximately 11,500 feet in central Colorado

tundra alpine region above treeline

wicking action which draws moisture away from its source; used in reference to clothing that promotes evaporation

About the Authors and Artist

RUTH and PETER FREY make their summer home in the Aspen area and have hiked the region's mountain trails since the late 1970s. When not in Aspen, Ruth prepares high school students for college entrance exams. Peter is a research scientist and university professor.

DONNA CURRIER is a free-lance illustrator who began her professional career in Denver. She applies her talents to a wide range of projects including magazine covers, art gallery catalogues, notecards, advertisements, and posters. Donna has worked as a courtroom artist and has created graphics for television.

Disclaimer

The trail descriptions in this book are based on conditions experienced by the authors in 1991 and 1992 and on information from topographic maps published by the U. S. Geological Survey. We have made every effort to be precise and accurate. Despite this, many of the conditions described are subject to change from year to year and even from month to month. Your experiences on these trails may be different from what we have described. Brush Creek Books and the authors do not warrant that the actual conditions on the trails will conform to our descriptions and maps. The book is only a guide and should be supplemented with current information from a reliable local source.

The acquisition of a hiking guide does not make you an expert. Colorado hikers must be wary of mountain weather and of the dangers of loose rock, snowfields, and hidden precipices. A careless step or an unheeded thunderhead can spell disaster. Brush Creek Books and the authors assume no liability for injury or accident. Our descriptions of these trails do not constitute an endorsement or recommendation.

TO:
BRUSH CREEK BOOKS
1317 Livingston Street
Evanston, IL 60201
(708) 328-2844

Please mail THE ASPEN DAYHIKER to the address below:

Name _____

Address _____

City/State/Zip _____

Telephone _____

I wish to order _____ copies of THE ASPEN DAYHIKER

I enclose $9.95 per book   total $ _____

I enclose $1.50 per book for postage & packaging   total $ _____

                                        TOTAL ENCLOSED $ _____

Please make checks payable to BRUSH CREEK BOOKS

TO:
BRUSH CREEK BOOKS
1317 Livingston Street
Evanston, IL 60201
(708) 328-2844

Please mail THE ASPEN DAYHIKER to the address below:

Name _____

Address _____

City/State/Zip _____

Telephone _____

I wish to order _____ copies of THE ASPEN DAYHIKER

I enclose $9.95 per book   total $ _____

I enclose $1.50 per book for postage & packaging   total $ _____

                                        TOTAL ENCLOSED $ _____

Please make checks payable to BRUSH CREEK BOOKS

Notes

Notes